CHANGE
LEADER

CHANGE LEADER

Learning to Do What Matters Most

Michael Fullan

JOSSEY-BASS
A Wiley Imprint
www.josseybass.com

Published by Jossey-Bass
A Wiley Imprint
989 Market Street, San Francisco, CA 94103-1741—www.josseybass.com

Grateful acknowledgment is made for permission to print the following:

Figure 3.1: "The Myth and the Reality of Change," by Herold, D. & Fedor, D., from *Change the way you lead change* (2008). Reprinted by permission of Stanford University Press.

Jossey-Bass books and products are available through most bookstores. To contact Jossey-Bass directly call our Customer Care Department within the U.S. at 800-956-7739, outside the U.S. at 317-572-3986, or fax 317-572-4002.

Wiley also publishes its books in a variety of electronic formats and by print-on-demand. Not all content that is available in standard print versions of this book may appear or be packaged in all book formats. If you have purchased a version of this book that did not include media that is referenced by or accompanies a standard print version, you may request this media by visiting http://booksupport.wiley.com. For more information about Wiley products, visit us www.wiley.com.

Library of Congress Cataloging-in-Publication Data
Fullan, Michael.
    Change leader : learning to do what matters most / Michael Fullan.
        p. cm.
    Includes bibliographical references and index.
    ISBN 978-0-470-58213-8 (cloth), 978-1-118-10657-0 (ebk), 978-1-118-10658-7 (ebk), 978-1-118-10659-4 (ebk)
    1. Leadership. 2. Organizational change. I. Title.
    HD57.7.F85 2011
    658.4'092—dc23
                                                                    2011017842
Printed in the United States of America

FIRST EDITION
HB Printing 10 9 8 7 6 5 4 3 2 1

CONTENTS

To Mary

All theory is against freedom of the will; all experience for it.

—Samuel Johnson, quoted in Boswell's *Life of Johnson*

PREFACE

THIS BOOK COMPLETES MY TRILOGY ON LEADERSHIP FOR Jossey-Bass. In *Leading in a Culture of Change* (2001) I focused on a framework of change that had five components: moral purpose, understanding change, relationship building, knowledge creation and sharing, and coherence making. In *The Six Secrets of Change* (2008) I dealt with six interrelated aspects: love your employees, connect peers with purpose, capacity building trumps judgmentalism, learning is the work, transparency rules, and systems learn. These two books are complementary. The first is more conceptual—although, as we shall see, I consider all the best concepts to be deeply experientially grounded. The second book is more strategic and gets at the practical theories of action that the most effective leaders engage in.

In the meantime I have been involved with several others in "doing" real change, especially whole-system reform, where we engage with practitioners and policymakers to bring about substantial improvements in large, complex education systems (Fullan, 2010a). It is this new work that is the genesis of this book, with those experiences reinforced by what is happening in some of the most successful, enduring organizations.

The more my colleagues and I grappled with change challenges, the more I realized that the most effective leaders use practice as their fertile learning ground. They never go from theory to practice or research evidence to application. They do it the other way around: they try to figure out what's working, what could be working better, and *then* look into how research and theory might help.

During this same period, a multibillion-dollar enterprise has burgeoned that is based on the promise of giving advice to leaders so that they can become more effective. The best leaders, as I said, take this advice with a grain of salt. Others, more needy, fall for it and try to figure out how to apply it. It doesn't work. It can't work, because these leaders are looking for answers in the wrong places. You can't find the answers outside yourself—you have to start inside and look for the best external connections to further develop your own thinking and action.

The best ideas are potentially right under our noses. You need to start with your own work, see how others in similar situations move forward, and create your own action plan using research and theory where they may help. In other words, use research and theory *selectively* in the service of practice. Research, theory, and management books are at best an input; at worst they are misleading, and great timewasters.

I recall being part of the examining committee in 1991 when Geoff Scott (now pro-vice chancellor at the University of Western Sydney, Australia) was defending his doctoral dissertation. At the end of the usual ritual, Geoff was asked the question, "Now that you have completed your dissertation and know what you know, is there anything you would have done differently?" Geoff must have been quite pleased with his performance up to that point because without hesitation he gave the rather gutsy response, "I would have used my brain."

Change Leader is about using your brain before it's too late. It presents a seven-part solution. First, it places practice front and center as the creative crucible. The remaining six elements consist of combining resolve, motivation, collaboration, confidence, impact, and "simplexity" (Kluger, 2008) (simple to understand, complex to make jell). The bonus is that the effective change leader will save a hell of a lot of time by not trying to decipher all that management advice—time put to better use in doing the real work of change. This book is about the wise practitioner rather than the abstract theorist; the reflective doer, not the smart operator; the deep accomplisher, not the overt hero. It may or may not have been Yogi Berra who said, "In theory there is no difference between theory and practice. In practice there is," but whoever said it was wise as well as witty. This book is about deep, practical practice, as simple as it is complex, and therefore achievable for anyone who wants to go for it.

Of course, I realize the irony. Mine is another management book. So it is caveat emptor—use your brain as you examine the ideas in this book in relation to your own practice and setting. As a change leader, you can figure out whether its ideas pan out in practice, skipping the empty question of whether they ring true to theory. At the very least my goal is to take the mystery out of complexity. Leadership is difficult because people are complicated and sometimes unmanageable. But you don't need fancy theory to tell you that. The answer, as we shall see, is much simpler, but not simplistic. The good news is that change leadership can be exercised effectively by anyone willing to learn a few core basics and then stick with them, getting better and better as they go. Practice-driven leadership, quite simply, is more accessible than theory-driven leadership. It takes us into the real world, where impressive empathy is more important than strategic plans, and where deliberate practice is the true hallmark of leadership. Deliberate practice is purposeful, action oriented, and reflective. It involves what I have called "motion leadership"—leadership that causes positive movement forward (Fullan, 2010b).

In essence this book is about how you can become your own change leader. It will give you the insights and ideas for how you can become more effective in what you do, and more influential in helping others change.

ACKNOWLEDGMENTS

I AM ENGAGED IN EXCITING CHANGE PROJECTS AROUND THE world, in work that is all about accomplishing bigger and better improvements. My colleagues in *Motion Leadership* and in *All Systems Go* are fantastic to work with, as we pursue what we call "whole-system reform"—how entire systems can get better and better.

We have recently begun to go more deeply into pedagogy by developing digital curricula that personalize and make learning exciting and intrinsically absorbing, and at the same time create the infrastructure and leadership necessary to make this new learning happen on a large scale. We call it "motion leadership meets madcap." Learning has never been so rewarding.

Among others, thanks to Eleanor Adam, Sir Michael Barber, Greg Butler, Claudia Cuttress, David Devine, MaryJean Gallagher, Andy Hargreaves, Ben Levin, Dalton McGuinty, Richard Mozer, Charles Pascal, Joanne Quinn, Sir Ken Robinson, Peter Senge, Lyn Sharratt, and Nancy Watson for making this journey increasingly fantastic.

Thanks further to Claudia Cuttress, mainstay of the creative and logistical infrastructure that guides our work. The superb editorial team from Jossey-Bass is terrific at both the big and the small stuff. Lead editor Lesley Iura proposed this book, supplied creative ideas throughout, and applied her wise editorial hand to improve the quality of the manuscript every step of the way. The result is immensely better because of Lesley. Thanks also to Justin Frahm of Jossey-Bass for shepherding the manuscript through the final production stages.

To Wendy, thanks for the sweet life at home, and for your loving and wise support in all our endeavors.

This book is dedicated to my mother, Mary—one of the greatest practitioners of the twentieth century who, as Minister of Finance in a family of seven boys, never went into deficit even though she had a paltry budget. She is one great practical exemplar.

ABOUT THE AUTHOR

MICHAEL FULLAN IS PROFESSOR EMERITUS AT THE ONTARIO Institute for Studies in Education at the University of Toronto, and is special adviser on education to Dalton McGuinty, the premier of Ontario.

Fullan is a doer and thinker. He served as dean of the faculty of education at the University of Toronto from 1988 to 2003, leading two major organizational transformations, including a merger of two large schools of education. He is currently working as adviser and consultant on several major education reform initiatives around the world. He holds honorary doctorates from The University of Edinburgh, Nipissing University in Ontario, and University of Leicester. Fullan bases his work on policy and practice drawn from both the public and private sectors, finding an increasing convergence in the best of this literature. He has written several best sellers that have been translated into many languages.

Visit his Web site at www.michaelfullan.ca.

CHANGE
LEADER

CHAPTER ONE
Practice Drives Theory

·CHAPTER TWO·
Be Resolute

·CHAPTER THREE·
Motivate the Masses

·CHAPTER FOUR·
Collaborate to Compete

·CHAPTER FIVE·
Learn Confidently

·CHAPTER SIX·
Know Your Impact

·CHAPTER SEVEN·
Sustain Simplexity

CHAPTER · ONE

Practice Drives Theory

Doing Is the Crucible of Change

To some, the notion that practice can be liberating while theory is confining may seem counterintuitive. Current practice does have a lot of built-in conservatism and inertia, but thinking and feeling practitioners are the only ones who can find ways to break through the inertia. To do so, they will need focus, coherence, and persistence—resources they will find far more readily in themselves (the feeling as well as the thinking parts) than in theory. Of course, research and theory can be useful, but only insofar as they help leaders move forward. Once you are free of the constraints of a new theory or past practice, you can explore multiple approaches, experiment, and above all *learn from your experience*. In this context, practice becomes a powerful tool for change.

Another fundamental reason that we need to ground our learning in practice is the growing research on how the brain works. Four findings stand out for our purposes. First, we are not always in control of our own thoughts because they come from the subconscious. Jacobs (2010) notes that "fMRI scans of our brains show that our perceptions

3

are a function of our feelings, desires, and memories" (p. ix)—and at the risk of being redundant, these phenomena occur *without our knowing that this is happening.* Let's call these "unpredictable inner drives." This means that learning about ourselves is a full-time job, and that we literally don't know ourselves unless we work at it. Chapter Five furnishes some ideas and self-learning exercises to help us learn and refine ourselves on an ongoing basis.

Second, if we are unpredictable and to a certain extent unaware of what motivates us, so is everyone else, by definition. Therefore as leaders we need to have what I call "impressive empathy," and manage others by creating environments that help them learn and grow. "Impressive empathy" includes understanding others who disagree with us—that is what makes it impressive!

Third, while being selfishly driven, so to speak, humans are also wired to connect. So-called "mirror neurons" cause us to be drawn to others (Goleman, 2006). While biologically (brain) driven to begin with, we consciously value the group once our relationships are cultivated. Beyond this most of us want to do good in this life and make a contribution, if we get that far—that is, if our self- and group learning gets that far.

Fourth, and most shockingly encouraging, is that our brain can be reshaped. Through *neuroplasticity*, we can engage in repeated new actions and thoughts that actually *forge and retain* new neural pathways. Thus, the brain can change its own structure and function through activity. We can learn, for example, to become more empathetic through repeated practice to the point that our empathy automatically kicks in because it becomes brain-wired (Doidge, 2007).

All of this is exciting and a bit daunting, but keeping with our simplexity principle, the good news is that we can become better leaders, and can help others become better by following a few powerful principles and strategies that are set out in this book. The bottom line is that your best source of learning is day-to-day practice because it is only experience that can engage and reshape the brain.

> **Key Insight 1**
>
> **The effective change leader actively participates as a learner in helping the organization improve.**

I argue in this book that most good ideas come from first examining good practices of others, especially practices that are getting results in difficult circumstances. The second step is to try out the new ideas yourself. The third entails drawing conclusions from what you have learned, and then expanding on those conclusions. Deliberative doing is the core learning method for effective leaders.

You will discover in this book seven key interrelated ideas and competencies that are essential for leading change through practice and experience: cultivating deliberative practice, being resolute, motivating others through linking to their realities, fostering collaboration, learning confidently, knowing your impact, and sustaining your learning from practice.

The result is that you will become a better change leader, and better at helping others and your organization change and become more effective. Most change initiatives fail. In the course of this book I will show that (1) you can't make people change (force doesn't work); (2) rewards are ineffective (buying superficial short-lived change at best); and (3) inspiration is not the driver we think it is (fails to reach enough people).

What does work is looking inside yourself and your practice as a full-time endeavor—and at the same time learning to relate to other people's realities while fostering collective capacity and identity. This book will show you what is entailed in doing this.

Caveat Emptor

Before getting into the nuts and bolts of the book, let's spend a moment looking at research and theory as they are currently presented to would-be change leaders. Management books by and large would have us start with expert advice—which, as it turns out, is abstract and inconsistent.

A good place to begin is Matthew Stewart's *The Management Myth: Why the "Experts" Keep Getting It Wrong* (2009). Stewart was finishing his doctoral dissertation on nineteenth-century German philosophy when he decided he needed a job. By his account, he went on a self-directed crash course of reading business books and the *Financial Times,* landed a job in an international management consulting firm, and began a rapid rise to high-priced consultant.

We can assume that Stewart's autobiographical sketch is a bit tongue-in-cheek and perhaps hyperbolic, but it rings more true to life than the grand theories. Many consultancy situations, he says, feature the same plot and characters: "the hapless client, the fiercely intelligent consultant, the unexpected insight, and the mutually profitable ending" (p. 17). The gist one gets from reading Stewart's account is that successful management consultants are people who make common sense complicated and then sell it well.

Stewart, of course, is not the first writer to attack the flimsy wisdom of management gurus. In *The Witch Doctors*, two staff editors from the *Economist*, Micklethwait and Wooldridge (1996), observed that "management theory" suffers from four defects:

> It is constitutionally incapable of self-criticism; its terminology usually confuses rather than educates; it rarely rises above common sense; and it is faddish and bedeviled by contradictions. (p. 13)

If anything, the situation has worsened in the past fifteen years. In 2004, Henry Mintzberg wrote a penetrating critique of MBAs in which he characterized the whole field as specializing in the "wrong people" engaged in promoting the "wrong ways" with the resulting "wrong consequences"—educationally, practically, organizationally, and societally (p. vii).

Mintzberg concludes that MBA graduates should have a skull and crossbones stamped firmly on their foreheads, over the words "Warning: NOT prepared to manage!" (p. 67), and characterizes what he calls "the impression left by MBA education" thusly:

1. Managers are important people who sit above others, disconnected from the work of making products and selling services.
2. Managing is decision making based on systematic analysis.

3. The data for such decision making comes from briefs, cases.

4. Under these managers sit their organizations, neatly separated . . . into the functions of finance, marketing, accounting, and so forth.

5. To bring these functions together, managers pronounce "strategies."

6. The best strategies are clear, simple, deliberate, and bold.

7. After these MBA managers have finished formulating their strategies, all the other people—known as "human resources"—must scurry around implementing them.

8. This implementation is, however, no easy matter, because although the managers who have been to business schools embrace change, many of those who haven't resist it.

9. To become such a manager, better still a "leader" who gets to sit on top of everyone else, you must first sit still for two years in business school. That enables you to manage anything. (2004, pp. 67–68)

Being irreverent, Mintzberg no doubt exaggerates, but the gist of his argument is sound—having theoretical analysts trained generically "to manage anything" or to advise others how to manage seems risky to say the least.

Then we have Pfeffer and Sutton's book (2006) *Hard Facts, Dangerous Half-Truths and Total Nonsense.* Their conclusion is essentially the same: "The advice managers get from the vast and ever-expanding supply of business books, articles, gurus, and consultants is remarkably inconsistent" (p. 33). They offer chapter and verse examples to make this point stick, but I'll spare you.

What we see time and again is that theory and strategy (abstract concepts) dominate practice and implementation (grounded concepts). Pfeffer and Sutton note that Google generates at least twice as many entries for the word *strategy* than for the word *implementation,* concluding that

> Judging by mentions on book titles and search engines, *figuring out what to do* seems to be far more important ... than *the ability to actually do something*—such as operate the business effectively. (2006, p. 135, italics in original)

Pfeffer and Sutton conclude that the least we can do is to slow the rate of adoption of bad practices (that is, taking bad advice). In studying four "good" versus four "bad" bank closings they found that "managers at each successful closing had largely ignored the procedures developed by the retail action team and developed their own practices instead" (p. 231). As they report, "One manager held up a thick book of procedures and policies put together by the retail action teams, and bragged that the key to his success was ignoring everything in the book!" By contrast, Pfeffer and Sutton found that "managers at each bad closing lamented that they had tried to follow the official procedures closely and doing so had hampered their ability to convince customers to transfer to other branches" (p. 231).

Unfortunately, if you think Pfeffer and Sutton might themselves have the answer, think again. Try reconciling their latest books, which they wrote separately. Sutton (2010) says, "be nice"; Pfeffer (2010) wants us to grab power. Sutton confidently claims that "treating people with dignity is what good bosses do" (p. 5). He has learned this "from a huge pile of academic studies during my 30-year career as a researcher and from thousands of observations and conversations with their bosses (and their colleagues) from workplaces of all kinds" (p. 7). Pfeffer proffers that "systematic research confirms that … being politically savvy and seeking power are related to career success and even to managerial performance" (p. 4). Likability is overrated, says Pfeffer; the irony may be too much when Pfeffer warns "beware of the leadership literature" (p. 11). (Of course you can find areas of commonality if you dig, such as that grit [perseverance and resilience] is essential for success, which I have to agree with—see Chapter Two in this book.)

On the education front, take a look at the head-scratching advice on performance or merit pay. Hanushek and Lindseth (2009), an economist and lawyer respectively, advocate performance pay for teachers with this lead-in: "There is *growing research* to show that rewarding successful teachers is one of the most important steps a school district can take to improve achievement…. A bipartisan group found that our current compensation system fails our teachers and our children. There it is, *pure and simple:* pay teachers based on their performance, as do virtually all other professions" (pp. 237–238, italics added).

Contrast that advice with what Pfeffer and Sutton have to say on the subject: "It turns out that merit pay for teachers is an idea that is almost 100 years old and has been the subject of much *research*." [They conclude], "*Evidence* shows … that merit pay consistently fails to improve student performance" (Pfeffer & Sutton, 2006, pp. 22–23, italics added).

There you have it, pure and simple—or a hundred years of research? Both conclusions smack of dead certitude. Each draws the opposite conclusion. In truth, you would be better off not to try to determine who is right, but rather to figure out for yourself what is right.

Of course, we can't blame management consultants for everything. And my point is not to discard management theories wholesale—in fact I have learned a lot from them over the years—just don't go seeking answers in books alone. Your own *reflective* practice is a more important tool. Books can be useful to tweak your reflections, but evidence (and the form in which it comes) is not how good leaders think. "A large percentage of expert advice is flawed," says Freedman as he compiles page after page of research studies in medicine, science, and business that turn out to be wrong (Freedman, 2010, p. 11). My book provides protection against bad advice because it helps change leaders learn to rely on themselves, including questioning themselves as they learn.

In my experience, effective change leaders—or any people who are successful in any walk of life—don't start with imagining the future. They walk into the future through examining their own and others' best practices, looking for insights they had hitherto not noticed. We will see examples of this sequence in action time and again throughout this book.

Effective leaders do not think and act like management gurus, and less effective leaders make matters worse for themselves and their organizations because they heed abstract management advice. It is not that typical management books contain *no* good ideas. It is just that these authors come at the solution the wrong way around. Practicing managers should first get in touch with and trust their own initial instincts. If you read a management book and find yourself agreeing with it but having no practical idea what to do, you should worry. If advice sounds too good to be true—or sounds like bunk—it probably is. If it comes from someone who has never actually managed a successful company, it is likely not sound advice about where and how to start.

Why Practice Needs to Drive

My claim in this book is to do the opposite of what most theories of management suggest—don't try to figure out someone else's theory but rather use practice to get at theory, and more directly use practice to discover strategies that work. The source of creative breakthroughs, then, is learning about and from practice, not theory.

William Duggan makes this same argument in *Strategic Intuition: The Creative Spark in Human Achievement* (2007). Like Mintzberg, he finds the concept of strategy wanting because it doesn't tell you where ideas come from in the first place. Reigning models of business strategy "leave out how strategists actually come up with their ideas" (p. 8). What Duggan finds is that the scientific method "depends not on imagination but on discovery" (p. 9), by which he means that you do not imagine or "theorize" the next creative idea, but rather you discover it through reflective practice and insight, and then develop it further.

Citing individuals from Copernicus to Gates and other creative breakthrough practitioners, Duggan illustrates how the paradigm for discovery is precisely the opposite of what we assume. For instance, in offering the breakthrough idea that the earth revolves around the sun, Copernicus

> did not come up with a new theory of physics. The new theory followed, with Newton, at the end of the scientific revolution. This sequence for a paradigm shift—from achievement then theory—is exactly backward from common ideas on how progress happens. (p. 17)

Our everyday manager is no Copernicus, but the sequence holds. If you want to improve practice, don't go to the business theorists. A better approach (adapting Duggan) is

Step 1. Examine your own practice and results and identify what might be lacking.

Step 2. Look in the laboratories of other practitioners in similar circumstances who seem to be achieving success.

Step 3. Building on Steps 1 and 2, try out something new in your own practice.

Step 4. If it works, draw a conclusion—your new theory—and do more of it, learning as you go.

In short, the new theory is the product of considered practice. It is not just that the change leaders immerse themselves in action, but rather they use it as the best source of evidence and insights. They do analyze, but their analysis is based on substance.

The good news, according to Duggan, is that "intelligent memory," as he calls it, is cumulative. Strategic intuition is "where past elements stored in memory combine in a flash of insight to give you an idea for action.... Strategic intuition projects intelligent memory into the future, as a course of action to follow, based solidly on the past" (p. 35). The brain, as I said earlier, rewires and retains subconsciously. The more experiential the source (that is, practice based), the greater the retention.

This stance of learning from practice—your own and that of others—is further reinforced by Johnson's fascinating historical sweep, *Where Good Ideas Come From* (2010). He shows time and again that new ideas come from loosely connected networks whereby "change leaders," let's call them, derive new ideas. We will return to Johnson's findings in Chapter Four, "Collaborate to Compete."

The creative premise for the change leader is not to "think outside the box" but to get outside the box, taking your intelligent memory to other practical boxes to see what you can discover. And if it makes sense and actually works in your situation, you have a new theory of action. This stance is enormously liberating for practitioners: you don't have to frustrate yourself and those around you with abstract theorizing.

Specific examples of effective change leadership along these lines are furnished in Chip and Dan Heath's book, *Switch: How to Change Things When Change Is Hard* (2010). The Heath brothers begin by drawing on Jon Haidt's "happiness hypothesis" (2006). Haidt suggests that we are governed by two forces that he dubs the Elephant (our emotional side) and the Rider (our rational side). The Elephant overpowers the Rider on most things. In other words, practice is more powerful than theory.

The trouble is that most practice is not very effective. The Elephant, if you like, takes the easy way out, favoring what is least taxing in the short term. When it comes to contemplating change "the Elephant is the one that gets things done" while "the Rider tends to overanalyze and overthink" (Heath & Heath, p. 8). The trouble is that if left alone the Elephant does the wrong things or nothing new, and the Rider thinks of some of the right things but only in theory. So the question I am addressing in the book you are holding is how to mobilize the energy of the Elephant and how to make the Rider's ideas more relevant to the task—or, to put it another way, how to achieve more effective practice through practitioners sharing ideas and influencing each other. We don't want to sideline the rational Rider, but rather enable her or him to think and act more effectively.

The Heaths cite several examples in their book. One case in point is the challenge that Jerry Sternin of the Save the Children fund faced when he was invited by the Vietnamese government to fight malnutrition in the country. Sternin did not start with theory—such as how to build sanitation systems and purify water, theories that he called TBU (true but useless).

Instead he started with practice, what he called "find the bright spots." He got together with groups of local mothers and organized teams to weigh and measure every child in their village. When they examined the results, Sternin asked, "Did you find any very, very poor kids who are bigger and healthier than the typical child?" By following up on the children who were healthier they discovered three things: "bright spot" moms were feeding their kids four meals a day instead of two (but the same amount of food); they fed the kids more actively (hand-fed); and most revealing, they were collecting tiny crabs and shrimp from the rice paddies and mixing them with the rice (Heath & Heath, pp. 28–30).

Six months after Sternin had arrived in Vietnam, 65% of the kids in the villages were better nourished and stayed that way. The program reached 2.2 million people in 265 villages. Note that it was not theory that changed the mothers' behavior. Nor, for that matter, would knowledge of nutrition, such as being told to add protein. For change to occur the mothers would "have to practice it" (Heath & Heath, p. 30) and thereby see the benefits. Time and again we find that effective change leaders cause people to act their way into new ways of thinking. The effective sequence involves mobilizing new practices that in turn lead to greater clarity and commitment.

A further validation of this way of approaching change (that is, action leads to better thinking) is found in Alan Deutschman's *Walk the Walk: The #1 Rule for Real Leaders* (2009). "Walking the walk" doesn't just mean actions speaking louder than words, but that you actually learn a lot more by doing. Deutschman shows throughout his book that when you walk the walk, you demonstrate what comes first, share in the struggle and the risk, and gain firsthand experience, thereby learning more about the issues. Every moment offers up-close opportunity to teach, train, and lead, and then others can see the steps you take.

Conversely, talking the talk will not inspire most people, and when it does the appropriate action still will not be clear. Leaders must be there as learners to generate the exceptional energy and persistence required for substantial change to occur. Talk is not convincing because ideas are not meaningful and memorable unless they stem from learning-based action.

The core qualities that Deutschman ends up with are exactly the qualities found in the practitioner change leaders that we will examine in subsequent chapters: resolve, motivation, collaboration, learning as you go, impact, and confidence. All of these factors involve learning through reflective action.

This emphasis on deliberately learning in action is captured beautifully in Pascale, Sternin, and Sternin's book *The Power of Positive Deviance* (2010). "Positive deviance" is about learning from successful exceptions. But it is more than that for our purposes; it is about learning with your boots on the ground. Pascale et al. strike at the essence of this approach when they state, "It's easier to act your way into a new way of thinking, than to think your way into a new way of acting" (p. 38). It is about "action" (behaving differently), and "consistency" (relentless focus). Moreover, it is about finding and learning from practice that works to solve extremely difficult problems. Sternin's experiment in reducing childhood malnutrition in Vietnam—without an influx of foreign aid money—is an example of one such solution.

Because their approach is based on hands-on examples of real-world problems, Pascale et al. are able to bring clarity to what may otherwise be mysterious management concepts. Take, for example, the attractive but elusive concept from

Heifetz and Linsky (2002) of "adaptive challenges" as distinct from "technical problems." The latter are problems for which we know the answers and the solution entails applying what we know. Adaptive challenges, by contrast, "require experiments, new discoveries and adjustments from numerous places in the organization and community. Without learning new ways—changing attitudes, values and behaviors—people cannot make the adaptive leap necessary to thrive in the new environment" (p. 13). I don't know about you, but I find this observation true but unhelpful.

In the hands of Pascale et al., because they are working on grounded problems, the concept of adaptive challenge becomes completely clear: The single thing that makes a problem adaptive is "*social complexity* and the need for *behavioral change*" (p. 49, italics in original). This I can understand. It is not that the problem is mysterious; it is more that helping people discover and embrace change is socially complex. Adaptive challenges and social complexity are one and the same.

Successful change is both simple and complex, what Kluger (2008) calls "simplexity." The simple part is that for most problems there are only a half-dozen or so key things you need to focus on. (We have seen this in our work in bringing about whole-system reform in education in changing 5,000 or more schools in Ontario [Fullan, 2010a].) Choose a small number of core priorities (in our case it was literacy, numeracy, and high school graduation), pursue them by building people's capacities in a nonjudgmental climate, and make sure you establish a two-way transparent learning relationship between practice and results. Simple to describe; difficult to execute.

The concept of simplexity is further evident in the study of how 20 of the most improved school systems in the world keep getting better conducted by Moursed, Chinezi, and Barber (2010) of McKinsey & Co. They found that a fine balance between capacity building and accountability interventions was required, along with knowing your starting point and adapting strategies according to context; for example, whether the situation was one of going from "awful to good," or from "good to great." Accountability-driven reforms use assessment of performance, punishment, and rewards, whereas capacity building invests in individual and group learning. You need both, but the change leader uses more of the latter than the former. We will see this social learning dynamic in Chapter Four whereby once capacity reaches a certain level, it is peers who become the main source of innovation. The change leader knows this and uses it for more growth in the organization.

The complex part in both the Ontario and McKinsey examples lies in the chemistry of making the half-dozen or so factors fuse in action—in getting people to change both individually and in concert. Simple list; complex combination.

The Change Leader

The themes in this book are not brand new; rather, they have become dormant over the past half-century as abstract theorizing has gained ascendancy. During that period the value of hands-on practical leadership has steadily declined in favor of distant CEOs and other professional managers. In a rather interesting take on the problem, Hopper and Hopper (2009) trace this to the loss of what they call "the Puritan Gift"—"a rare ability to create organizations that serve a useful purpose, and to manage them well" (p. xxiii). They argue that we underplay domain-specific knowledge and fail to appreciate not only the practical but also the *intellectual* quality of hands-on work. Being an effective manager involves clever work, learned through reflective doing.

I would mount a similar critique with respect to what has happened over the past fifty years in my own field, education. We have lost the capacity to build effective practice through the teaching profession and its leaders. Instead we have politicians running around introducing ad hoc policies far removed from practice that have no chance of improving practice on the ground.

Ever since formal policy and research (that is, theories distant from practice) became a prominent part of finding a solution—from 1965 onward—the United States has declined from being number one in the world in educational attainment to its current status of about 24th despite having tripled its per-pupil expenditures in real dollars over the same time period (Goldin & Katz, 2008; Cohen & Moffitt, 2009).

The decline, I believe, is a function of superficial, silver-bullet solutions that actively disregard and disrespect practice. The point is not that practice is always good, but rather how to *improve it.* Matthew Crawford (2009)—a PhD in political philosophy who also likes to work on motorcycles—describes how hands-on practice can be both more interesting and more productive. He finds "manual work more engaging *intellectually*" (p. 5, italics in original).

"The truth does not reveal itself to idle spectators," says Crawford (p. 98). In other words, hands-on work has more *meaning*. With a direct connection, you care more, and you must be simultaneously technical and deliberative: "You come up with an imagined train of causes for manifest systems and judge their likelihood before tearing anything down" (p. 25). When you do this work in conjunction with other practitioners, it also becomes more socially engaging. Such work is cognitively and socially more intrinsically rewarding, and more effective for addressing the problems at hand.

The advice for change leaders that we have established thus far is to dwell on your own situation and practice—as well as that of other practitioners—as a basis for action. Draw continuously on outside ideas but always in relation to how they relate to your situation, and how it could be improved. Mintzberg (2009) takes the same stance when he urges that "after years of seeking those Holy Grails, it is time to recognize that managing is neither a science nor a profession; it is a practice, learned primarily through experience, and rooted in context" (p. 9).

More and more it appears that you don't have to be a superstar to be effective; rather you need to work on being a clear-headed, persistent learner in the setting in which you work, with an eye to the bigger picture. For example, you don't have to read a hundred books to know that effective management is about people. Stewart (2009) captures this as well as anyone:

> A good manager is someone ... with a wide knowledge
> of the world and an even better knowledge of the way
> people work; someone who knows how to treat people with
> respect; someone with honesty, integrity, trustworthiness,
> and other things that make up character; someone in short

who understands oneself and the world around us well enough to make it better. (p. 303)

But the question for us is how to achieve those characteristics. The answer can be found in what Colvin (2008) calls "deliberate practice." The vast majority of us are not born with talent; it must be developed. And it is not theory that develops talent, nor is it mere experience (twenty years doing the same thing is just one year's experience times 20). Colvin, claiming that "talent is overrated," documents that the best people in any business or sport are those who put in the effort to train and learn from their experience. And it's not easy. The ten-year rule really is true: it takes years of continuous application and learning to become an expert.

The characteristics of deliberate practice include the following:

- It can be repeated, a lot.
- Feedback on performance and results is continuously available.
- It is highly demanding mentally.
- It isn't much fun when you are learning it. (Colvin, 2008)

Through deliberate practice, your task is to deepen your knowledge about what works and about how to support and develop others, including the particular others with whom you are working. The most attractive and the best organizations are those that have a reputation for developing people. By definition they have leaders who are good at their own development and establishing the environment whereby they help others learn and grow. But how to get this good is tricky. Strange as it sounds, *accomplishment* can generate greater moral purpose than trying to increase moral purpose directly.

Passion and vision are long-standing pillars in the house of management, at least since Tom Peters went searching for them over thirty years ago. But it turns out they are not the "drivers" we thought they were. When passion comes alive—when it turns out to be a powerful driver—it is in situations where we actually accomplish something of high moral value, which in turn energizes us to do even more. I have called this "realization" (Fullan, 2011a). It is the being in the moment of a successful endeavor that fuels passion, not the dreaming of it. Thus, exhorting people to have greater moral commitment is often less effective than helping them get new experiences that activate their moral purpose. The establishment of new practices and experiences galvanizes passion. This is the essence of *the change leader:* the capacity to generate energy and passion in others through action.

This book helps the change leader become more effective by providing a framework and examples wherein practice is the driver. It would be inconsistent for me to claim that all you need to do is to master the seven factors that I highlight. But I will argue that we have a good case of simplexity here. The simple part is that the seven themes are easy to grasp one by one. The complex part is getting good at applying them in combination. Your job, then, is to use deliberate practice as a way to learn the craft of change while fostering it in members of your organization. Do that, and you can solve today's problems while simultaneously shaping the next generation of

Figure 1.1: The Change Leader

leaders. The richest source of learning is through the alchemy of application.

Figure 1.1 shows the relationship of the seven elements of change leadership. Start with building up and cultivating your commitment to stay the course, what I called **being resolute**. The outer foundation for the work of the change leader is **deliberate practice** and **sustained simplexity** (not too simple, not too complex). As you incorporate these elements into your daily practice, you begin to **motivate** those you are leading and encourage **collaboration** and constructive **competition** to build capacity. Because you are immersed in the action, where ideas are being generated, you **learn** a great deal. And because what you and others learn is concrete, you and they gain **confidence**. Nonetheless, you double-check this all the time by establishing mechanisms that allow you to **know your impact.** These mechanisms serve to demonstrate accountability to the outside and to provide feedback for improvement.

Of course, this is all an oversimplification, but ideally it provides an overview of how these seven elements interact in concert and how you as leader can both guide the process and learn from the dynamics. Subsequent chapters will furnish plenty of examples of how these elements work in practice.

The change leader framework is not a guide to action, but rather a tool to foster deliberate practice: apply, learn, get feedback on results, do more, and so on. Being resolute (Chapter Two) is the driving force that flows throughout several of the other elements: empathetic relationship building (Chapter Three); collaborative focus (Chapter Four); becoming a confident (but humble) learner (Chapter Five); and continually measuring and learning from the impact you and others are having (Chapter Six). The qualities that hold all this together are deliberate practice and sustained simplexity (simple to understand, complex to make jell).

My advice from the beginning of this chapter applies to my ideas as well as those of others: be a critical consumer. Examine received wisdom in light of your own practice and that of your peers, and only after thorough consideration of that practice. This framework does put the onus on you as change leader. If practice is going to drive improvement, the leader's job is to liberate practice. Machiavelli said it best 500 years ago, "A prince who is not himself wise cannot be well advised" (1515, 1961). The goal is to be both wise and well advised by your own and others' practice. It will take time.

CHAPTER · TWO

Be Resolute

Act with Purpose and Empathy

In this chapter we see how resolute leadership benefits the organization, how "impressive empathy" (the ability to understand others who disagree with you) is crucial, and how you as a change leader need to understand what it takes to get this good. The key insight for this chapter is

Key Insight 2

Effective change leaders combine resolute moral purpose with impressive empathy.

We always knew that resolute action was essential but now we have come to appreciate the critical role of impressive empathy. The latter is empathy for others who disagree with you, those who are, in a word, *in your way*. Of course there will be situations where you must fire people or otherwise overcome them. But successful change comes when the masses get involved. And when you get numbers of people involved there will always be some who are either against the direction or apathetic. Your job is to overcome reticence and opposition—what we have come to call "the moral imperative realized" (Fullan, 2011a; Sharratt & Fullan, 2009).

Because change is hard, all effective leaders are driven by resolute purpose with respect to deep human values. They simply do not, and would never, give up. The change insight here is that blind resolution is not enough. In order for their persistence to pay off, leaders also have to possess the impressive empathy that enables them to understand where people who disagree are coming from, and thus figure out how to relate to them. What is "impressive" is the ability to put yourself in other people's shoes, particularly those who hold values and experiences very different than yours. We will look at this later in the chapter. Without impressive empathy there is no other way to reach such people.

Staying the Course: How the Organization Benefits

If you take away nothing else from this chapter, remember two things: (1) when you are on a crucial mission, stay the course against all odds; and (2) be impressively empathetic when it comes to opposition in the early stages. Staying the course is seen in all long-term successful companies. Leaders in sustained successful organizations focus on a small number of core priorities, stay on message, and develop others toward the same end, making corrections as new learning occurs.

In 1999, Bill Hogarth, the director of education in the York Region District School Board, just north of Toronto, stunned the school system when he said that all York children should be reading by the end of grade 1. Mobilizing 9,000 teachers and 130,000 students in 190 schools is no small change feat. Ten years of widespread resolute leadership later, York Region has pretty much accomplished that ambitious goal and is going deeper.

A resolute leader does not work single-handedly. Rather, using their change savvy such leaders spawn focused determination throughout the organization by mobilizing and developing others in the organization. Take Ryan Friedman, for example, one of a hundred or more school leaders in York Region that I could have selected who were encouraged and cultivated by Bill Hogarth.

Friedman was the principal of Crosby Heights Elementary School with 660 students in a low-income neighborhood. When he began as principal in 2004 the school culture was toxic, the building dilapidated, and staff morale at sub-basement levels. Management and the teachers' union were involved in constant battles, and many parents were looking for another school for their children.

Friedman's personal vision included several broad principles that demonstrated his determination to address the school's problems:

- Learning for all, whatever it takes
- All equals *all*
- Discover and foster student and staff potential
- A focus on literacy
- Excellence in all that we do

He also had a number of other particular objectives, such as establishing a job-embedded learning culture. But as important as his goals was Friedman's resolve: he modeled hope, optimism, high expectations, and caring for others, especially when things were bad. He pushed forward while also consistently maintaining empathy for those who were skeptical, until most people came on board. For example, when union leaders and others were wary of his first endeavors, he did not attempt to convince them with evidence or overpower them with moral purpose or authority. Instead he empathized and created the conditions for success. He was persistent but patient. He modeled the goals and values he was expecting in others. He made time and resources available for developing new capacities. He showed how the new practices were getting results. He created a climate of high challenge/high support.

Ryan Friedman also demonstrated another quality that we have seen in our motion leadership work and is a facet of impressive empathy. If you want to have any chance of changing a negative relationship you have to give other people respect *before they have earned it*. For example, if a leader enters a negative culture, as Friedman did, he will encounter a situation in which people have, so to speak, learned to be disrespectful. Thus they will not give you respect on day one. You have to model and demonstrate respect (as well as do other things to move the organization forward) even when it is not being reciprocated. This is hard to do, but confident change leaders are able to pull this off.

Friedman and his staff accomplished astonishing results within three years. Reading and writing proficiency on the province's rigorous standards assessment more than doubled, going from 44 to 90% and from 40 to 87%, respectively;

math scores went from 50 to 83% (Sharratt & Fullan, 2009). Resolution pays off. It was not because of one leader—Ryan Friedman—but because the entire organization—York Region District—hired, promoted, and supported such leaders.

In the best cases resolute leadership is a system quality. Identical leadership qualities are found in successful organizations in any sector—focused determination along with resilience and the development of leadership throughout the organization is the winning combination. The Mayo Clinic has seen over a hundred years of success and growth by implementing these qualities. The Clinic was founded in 1889 by Dr. William Worrall Mayo and his two sons, Drs. Will and Charlie Mayo. By 1908 it was known as the Mayo Clinic and had 12 physicians; today it has 2,500 on three campuses. The most recent chief administrative officer, Shirley Weis, observes, "What makes Mayo Clinic work today is the fact that physicians here understand it is *their* practice" (Berry & Seltman, 2008, p. 101, italics original).

The Mayo brothers and their successors didn't get this good by reading management books. Rather, these leaders focused on their practice and used outside innovations (such as the use of information technology and ideas to utilize data effectively) selectively in service of the practice.

Mayo is resolute about developing resolute leaders:

Mayo Clinic's senior leaders have few worries about the next generation of Clinic leaders. In fact, two generations of future leaders are mostly on campus today, and they are being deliberately readied for senior leadership positions . . . . This speaks to two important commitments. First, Mayo's commitment to find internal talent to sustain the values, culture, and clinical model that has proven to be effective for so long. . . . Second, Mayo has a commitment to deliberately cultivate physicians and high-level administrative leaders [who work in teams]. (Berry & Seltman, 2008, p. 243)

Like any great organization, Mayo has a systematic career and leadership program within the organization. It is based on three modules: (1) Mayo Clinic heritage; (2) individual and personal development; (3) team development. The program is offered to four groups: newly appointed staff, newly appointed leaders, experienced leaders, and senior leadership (Berry & Seltman, p. 245).

Once again resolute leadership is a built-in *organization* quality, not an individual happenstance. And it works. The Mayo Clinic leads all other U.S. providers according to objective measures of outcomes about safety, service, preventable death, mortality rates, and adverse events with harm to the patient (Berry & Seltman, p. 229).

Gittell (2009) found the same phenomenon in her comparative study of hospitals. Hospitals that were effective had what Gittell called "relational coordination." The latter consisted of two sets of qualities built into the culture of the organization. The first set related to "relationships," specifically "shared goals, shared knowledge, and mutual respect." The second set concerned "communication" that was "frequent and timely" and oriented to ongoing "problem solving." These qualities were built up and sustained in the organization by leaders over many years—focused persistence once more.

What difference does relational coordination make? Put bluntly, if you were admitted to a hospital with low relational coordination your chances of dying would be greater. Relational coordination depends on leadership of the very kind we are identifying throughout this book. Higher performance health care, she found, depends on "leadership for change":

> We have found significant gaps in the high performance work systems in the hospitals we studied. What we observed over and over again were not just random gaps in those hospitals' work systems but repeated failure to extend those systems fully to physicians. Whether it was selection for teamwork, measuring performance broadly, rewards for teamwork, conflict resolution, patient rounds, or clinical pathways, physicians were the least likely of any care provider discipline to be included in cross-functional, high performance work practices.... [Yet] a more effective change process is one led by physicians who embrace the values of collaborative systems. (Gittell, 2009, pp. 234–235)

Those hospitals that did establish a leadership for change system performed significantly better than health care organizations that failed to do so. As Gittell notes, it is not enough for health care organizations (or any organization) "to have highly skilled committed employees; their employees must be able to coordinate their actions intelligently with one another, and on the fly" (p. 51). We will see more of this coordination in action in subsequent chapters, but my point here is that such deep, impressive organizational qualities can only be established by leaders who stay the course on this deep agenda.

Two other remarkable examples exemplify the crucial combination of resolute leaders who also develop others in the core task of developing successful learning organizations. One comes from the hotel industry, the other from the field of arctic exploration. I take these up in turn.

Isadore Sharp, the son of poor immigrants from Poland, was born in Toronto in 1931. Today he is the founder and chairman of one of the world's most admired and successful hotel brands in the world, Four Seasons. Like all successful resolute leaders he combines focus, higher-order purpose, and the development and engagement of all those who work in the organization. Sharp (2009) built the business based on four pillars: quality, service, culture, and brand (p. xvi). He opened his first hotel in Toronto in 1961. By 2008 Four Seasons had 82 hotels in 34 countries, and is still growing. All through the almost half-century period, with all the financial ups and downs, Four Seasons has been loyal to its employees, to quality service, and has never lowered its rates even in the toughest of times. What accounts for this impressive track record in such a highly competitive worldwide industry?

The answer is resolute leadership, unwavering focus on quality, and continuous extension of these values to managers and employees throughout the company. Sharp's treatment of quality is a good example of basing his decisions on practice. He says "quality control" is a misnomer, because "it can't be installed through elaborate appraisal systems, inspection systems, or quality training" (Sharp, 2009, p. 91). He follows a simple principle: treat others as you would like to be treated, which he applied to employees and customers alike. He centered his belief and actions on the premise that "we should be treating our employees the same way as we expect them to treat our customers" (p. 93). Not leaving this message to chance or only to training, he focused on practice: "At all my visits to all my hotels, I kept restating our aim of superior service focusing employees at every level—and, I hoped, management—on one simple compelling purpose: pleasing customers" (p. 93).

Sharp, in those he hired and in relentless day-to-day communication and action, sold and resold the culture of quality and service. This culture, says Sharp, must be evident in every nook and cranny of the organization: clerks, bell staff, bartenders, waiters, cooks, housekeepers, and dishwashers—the lowest paid and, in most companies, the least motivated people, but the ones who can make or break a five-star operation (p. 98). The insights of the change leaders come into play when Sharp says that you need to "delegate authority as well as responsibility"(p. 98), and you need "a workforce that willingly and immediately solved its own problems as they arose" (p. 99). Sharp found that the biggest problem was getting managers within the company to realize that the company's credibility among employees was crucial:

> Many of our managers paid considerable attention to our public image but few considered our image within the company: how our employees saw their managers, which I considered equally important, for without complete rapport between the top and the bottom, complete rapport with our customers was impossible. (p. 100)

So Sharp set out to build managers who reflected and practiced the four core pillars (quality, service, culture, and brand). Extending the circle of leaders throughout the organization who act with common purpose is the key to systemwide success. It took five years to get the degree of consistency that he was seeking, but once it reached a critical mass it began to have self-generating qualities. Just as in the Mayo Clinic, leaders are always developing the next generation of leaders as they do today's work. Four Seasons hires more for attitude than experience, cultivates and promotes from within, and its leaders are more likely to live their values rather than just talk about them.

The core values of effective resolute leaders have a moral quality. Sharp emphasizes that the Golden Rule for him is that "all people are equal in our eyes, whether guests or employees" (2009, p. 235), which he underscores by saying, "we could go anywhere in the world and bring together a core group of people from the community who could rise to this level of excellence in service and delivery" (p. 235). The true competitive advantage of Four Seasons, argues Sharp, is the alignment of corporate and human values, because it is through such continuous focus that you get collective engagement and wisdom as a result of all levels of the organization acting in concert.

With less detail and in an entirely different realm, we can appreciate the power of reflective determination in the Antarctic explorer Ernest Shackleton. Almost a hundred years ago Shackleton and 27 men set out for the Antarctic in their ship, *Endurance*. They got halfway to the South Pole when they were choked off by ice and lost their ship. They were over 1,000 miles from civilization with no means of communication. They set off in what was to be an incredibly difficult journey over ice floes. Eventually, Shackleton and five others sailed in a small lifeboat over 800 miles of open water in order to get help.

Almost two years after the expedition began all 28 men were rescued, surviving in good health. Two business writers, Morrell and Capparell (2001), capture Shackleton's leadership qualities.

We see his determination, reflective learning, and empathy: you make a decision to "stick through the tough learning period, ... cultivate a sense of compassion for others, ... [and] learn from past mistakes" (p. 45). Morrell and Capparell also show how Shackleton selected and developed talent and dealt with crises by staying open to others' ideas, listening, showing confidence, and defusing tension. The most successful leaders seem to be able to combine authority and democracy seamlessly. Accountability gets built into the culture as people individually and collectively take responsibility whether the leader is present or not.

We see many of the above core qualities in our own work that involves studying and helping to turn around school systems. In Ontario, for example, we have been pretty successful in transforming the public school system since 2003 from its previous five years of stagnation. The population of Ontario is 13 million, and there are 2 million students in the public school system in 4,000 schools based in 72 districts.

Ontario Premier Dalton McGuinty epitomizes resolute leadership. In a recent speech in Washington, D.C., he talked about seven lessons he goes by, three of which are pertinent to resolute leaders:

- The drive to make progress in our schools can't be a fad.
- Education reform is not important to your government unless it's important to the head of your government—personally.
- If you want to achieve your goals, you need to keep up the pressure all the time. (in Fullan, 2010a, p. 64)

Having been warned that Tony Blair lost the educational plot in his second term as prime minister (that is, Blair failed to continue the core focus on literacy and numeracy in 2001 after his successful first term in office), McGuinty, upon being reelected in 2007, declared that he was intensifying and deepening the plot. Persistence pays off. Ontario's literacy and numeracy scores on its demanding annual assessment have risen 14%; high school graduation has climbed from 68 to 81% and is still rising; and Ontario does very well internationally, having been recognized by McKinsey & Co. (Mourshed, Chinezi, & Barber, 2010) as one of the top-performing school systems in the world that "keep getting better" (along with Singapore, Hong Kong, and South Korea).

With resolute leadership at the whole-system level, local leadership can thrive. We have already seen a glimpse of this in Ontario through Bill Hogarth and Ryan Friedman in York Region. Ottawa Catholic District School Board also demonstrates the payoff of focused, persistent leadership. Jamie McCracken, the director (CEO) of the district, had been a high school principal in the district and had worked at the district office. He describes the culture of the district back then as "clenched." The system had 12 or so "thrusts" annually that served as priorities, but since there was little follow-through or continuity, not much changed. Jamie was hired to change that culture in the district's 82 schools housing some 42,000 students.

Being focused and resolute, he conducted two "re-imagining days" with all staff after which he promptly announced that there would be only three priorities: success for students, success for staff, and stewardship of resources. These three priorities have remained the same for the seven years he was director. How is the district doing? On all objective measures of student achievement they have performed steadily better over the seven years, now being the highest-performing large school districts in the province (see Fullan, 2010a).

In short, resolute leadership focusing on developing others engaged in a common cause characterizes all these successful organizations.

Impressive Empathy

If they are not careful, resolute leaders can be blind to the human dynamics that stand in their way. In fact, one could make a case that the greater their determination, the *less* effective leaders are in establishing lasting reform. We could cite countless examples over time, but let's take the case of Michelle Rhee, the courageous chancellor of the District of Columbia Public School System. Tackling a turgid bureaucracy and embedded unionism in a school system that continually failed to serve its children, Rhee focused on student achievement, fired over 200 low-performing teachers, closed schools, and introduced merit pay. She spent a tumultuous three-year tenure only to be forced to resign when the political fortunes (inevitably) changed. Maybe nobody could have succeeded in that situation, but it is clear that empathy, impressive or otherwise, was not Rhee's strong suit, and, once again, we see that "being right" is not a strategy. Rhee is admirable but my point is that she was *bound to fail*, getting at best short-term victories. Most significant, for our purposes, her leadership produced almost no ownership on the part of the people necessary for success—nor could it have. The more things change, the more they remain the same.

Lest you think I am being unduly hard on Rhee, let us consider an even more daunting example of a leader who had to confront even greater problems but acted differently. As a leader, how would you go about facing down a long history of racism in a formerly segregated university department in the first years of post-apartheid South Africa? This was the challenge that Jonathan Jansen took on a decade ago. In 2001, Jansen, a black man, was appointed as the dean of the Faculty of Education of South Africa's University of Pretoria which had just been combined with Teachers Training College Pretoria the year before. His first day on the job, Jansen pulled up to the parking lot gate and said, "Good evening comrades. I am the new dean of education; can I get my keys?" The two white gate attendants doubled over in laughter. "Yeah," said one of them, "and I am Bishop Tutu."

Later on in the first year, Jansen and his 13-year-old daughter were walking through a shopping center one Saturday morning, when he spotted a white colleague walking in the opposite direction:

> I brightened up, moved slightly in her direction, and greeted her heartily in Afrikaans: "Good morning Michelle." She refused to make eye contact, looking down and moving along at a steady pace. This must be a mistake, I thought. Perhaps she did not hear or see me. I tugged my daughter further in her direction and raised my voice, this time greeting even more loudly. She looked at me quickly, quickened her step, and moved determinedly ahead without greeting. "I don't think she knows you," said my daughter. "But she does," I insisted to myself.... Just the day before we had been part of a long meeting; as a senior administrator

she took the minutes, but also contributed some technical information. That *was* Michelle. (Jansen, 2009, p. 145, italics original)

Jansen recounts similar stories of the discrimination that he faced all through his life. Despite this personal history of being on the receiving end of institutionalized racism, Jansen understands and empathizes with white Afrikaners' past as "one of bitter struggle against the colonialists, the English, and the Communists." He recognizes that "their knowledge of the past is one of the Anglo-Boer wars and the desperate poverty that followed" (p. 46). He describes giving a speech to a group of white high school students in an all-girls school, talking about the need to cross bridges never crossed before. In the question period, one white girl asked without hostility, "Well, Professor, I agree with what you say about crossing bridges and stuff. But tell me this, how do I cross bridges toward someone who looks like the people who almost killed my sister and me a few weeks ago in a violent car hijacking?" (p. 90).

As Jansen recounts these and other experiences he had in trying to further the rights and presence of black students and black faculty in the university, he comes to this astounding conclusion: "I realize for the first time that these children are my children and that I will spend all my energy to help them [white students] make the transition across this difficult bridge" (p. 93). Jansen does this not because he is a nice guy (which he is) but rather *because he wants change.*

Jansen is no pushover. He is resolute. He takes strong stands. "In the case of the lecturer who intersperses her teaching with snide racial comments about the capability of black students," he makes it clear that this is not acceptable and that continuation of racial insult will lead to dismissal. When two senior high school principals come to see him about the instruction being delivered in English at the university rather than Afrikaans, he tells them that this is a South African university, not an Afrikaans university, and that both English and Afrikaans would be the languages of instruction, and the sooner they get used to the idea the better.

He fought tooth and nail, and within a short period black students constituted 45% of the residential student body and 65% of the total enrollment. When Jansen finished his term as dean in 2007, the University of Pretoria Faculty of Education was a much different place—a legacy of discrimination seriously undermined in six years. Jansen concludes that a "leader must have credibility [with both groups] to convince black and white students and black and white staff to even consider the possibility of crossing over" (2009, p. 273).

When it comes to deep divisions, resolution and empathy must be combined if change is to occur. The change leader knows that he or she must alter both motivation and capacity, and that both staying the course and impressive empathy will be required. Resolute leaders like Jansen prevail not just because they are determined, but also because of the way they go about their work. They are confidently hopeful "no matter what." Duggan (2007) talks about Susan B. Anthony and her tireless pursuit of women's suffrage. After 54 years of relentless effort she gave a speech in 1906 on her eighty-sixth birthday with the title "Failure Is Impossible." She was right, although she didn't live to see the result of her conviction. She died within four weeks, and women won the right to vote only fourteen years later, in 1920.

Resolute leaders really do believe that failure is impossible, and they act that way, sometimes succeeding in their own time or through those that follow. They end up accomplishing things under circumstances that seem incredible. In Chapter One, we saw the simple, elegant example of how Jerry Sternin increased the health of Vietnamese children by looking for "bright spots" in which some poor mothers were getting success using very ordinary ideas in feeding their children (Heath & Heath, 2010). Additional examples are reported in Pascale and colleagues' examination (2010) of positive deviance (focusing on positive exceptions to the norm). Pascale and his colleagues use examples of harrowing problems to analyze success in social change: female genital mutilation in Egypt; childhood malnutrition; infant mortality; and, in Uganda, outcast girls who had formerly been abducted by guerillas forced into sexual slavery, and sometimes forced to kill their own family members. Here the empathy is not for the "bad guys" but for ordinary people who are coming up with solutions to seemingly impossible problems. The change leader in this case does not go for expert solutions (which are in all probability not implementable), but tries to find "deviant" small examples of success, and in turn extracts and leverages them for wider success.

Leaders with empathy do not see people's behavior as necessarily fixed. Their empathy tells them that perhaps the behavior is *situational:* if you want to change people's behavior, change the situation. With behavioral changes, however, it is important that the change be simple—or at least doable without complexity. For example, as we will see in Chapter Six, the simple use of checklists can have enormous impact, as Gawande (2010) proved in his work with physicians. Doctors and nurses merely washing their hands regularly saves thousands of lives. You just change the situation by making it easy to do the new thing (although this requires careful monitoring at the beginning). In many cases, say the Heaths (2010), what looks like a people problem is actually a situational problem. The bottom line is that empathetic leaders are more likely to recognize this type of problem, and thus are more likely to discover solutions that address the experiences of people involved. Ultimately, this can bring about change that the people themselves embrace.

Becoming a Resolute Change Leader

Are resolute leaders born or made? Well, judging from their abundant presence in certain organizations that deliberately cultivate such leadership, they are made. But let's start with how individual leaders themselves get that good.

I introduced Colvin (2008) in the previous chapter. He argues that innate talent (being born with it) is overrated and that the vast majority of those who get better do so by working on the capacities or skills in question. Mozart became Mozart "by working furiously hard" (p. 29). He takes Jerry Rice, the greatest wide receiver in NFL history, and shows that he got that way by working harder in practice and in the off-season than anyone else. In so doing he spent very little time playing football, compared to practicing; he designed his practice to work on his specific needs; while he was supported by others, he did much of his work on his own; and it wasn't always fun (pp. 54–57).

If you want to become a successful change leader it is up to you. You can improve, immensely so, by working on it. Again, take the ten-year rule: it requires ten years of deep development to become an expert in anything—including change management. And then you have to keep learning. Both Colvin (2008) and Dweck (2006) show that it is not fixed talent but mindset and situational learning that make the difference. People with a fixed mindset see mistakes as negative and try to avoid mistakes or hide them. For resolute learners "it's not about immediate perfection. It's about learning something over time: confronting a challenge and making progress" (Dweck, p. 24).

Dweck continues, "Fixed mindset leaders, like fixed mindset people, in general live in a world where some are superior and some are inferior" (p. 112). If others fail it is because they are not capable—not much room for empathy there! It is revealing that they need to protect themselves if what they are leading does not succeed by blaming either others or circumstances (bad luck).

Opposite to this is Dweck's theory of "growth mindset," which is fundamentally congruent with the thesis of my book: you learn through practice. You look for and seek growth in yourself and in others. Your attitude toward mistakes is completely different from the attitudes of those with fixed mindsets. You expect to learn from mistakes. You believe that there is room for improvement in yourself and in others.

Colvin's point and mine is that the vast majority of us can substantially improve our leadership by focusing on learning and putting in the time—growth is the name of the game. For a change leader, being resolute incorporates two closely related elements: organizational focus, and an emphasis on developing your own leadership and that of others.

With regard to the first element, focus, we have already seen in this chapter that organizations that work on a small number of core priorities and stay the course in learning how to get better and better at accomplishing them generally are more successful. This requires resolute leaders. Frenetic pacesetters—we are going to innovate, try and keep up with us—are bad for the organization. In education, our colleague Doug Reeves (2010) calls this "the law of innovation fatigue"—a constant stream of initiatives, each of which might make sense in its own right but that collectively add up to a fragmented system where nothing gets accomplished. In contrast, effective change leaders help the organization focus and learn over time.

Concerning the second element, for the change leader as an individual the message is to develop your own talent over time even though you might go from one organization to another. With this growth mindset you will get better and better as a change leader. There is thus a double payoff. The organization you are leading is more successful, and you become more effective. Put yourself in the situation of learning from others, and help them learn.

Nothing is fixed. You can change the situation and grow the talent—your own and that of others. The problem is that not enough organizations are "making" such leaders; that is, there are not enough resolute, empathetic leaders at the top who see their main job as hiring and cultivating critical masses of other focused leaders. Resolute leaders apply their persistence with empathy, and it is the latter that enables their resoluteness to pay off, because they reach and thereby motivate more people. Motivating people, after all, is what change is about. And it is the hardest of all change agent skills to learn. Be resolute, demonstrate impressive empathy, and motivate the masses.

CHAPTER·THREE

Motivate the Masses
Experiencing Is Believing

You can't make people change, and rewards and punishment either don't work or are short lived—the only thing that works is people's intrinsic motivation, and you have to get at this indirectly.

So far we have looked at deliberate practice as the crucible of learning, and empathetic resolute leadership committed to making learning better and better. But what is going to motivate the masses? Impressive empathy is a start, but you also need something to actually engage people. The big change problem, then, is how to get people to put in the energy to improve a situation when a lot of them don't want to do it. How do you get people to change their minds? Grasping the essence of quality change processes is the focus of this chapter.

Machiavelli had it right five hundred years ago. When people contemplate new ideas, he observed, they are "generally incredulous, never really trusting new things unless they have tested them by experience" (1515, 1961). The key word here is *experience*. Grasping change involves giving people new experiences that they end up finding intrinsically fulfilling. Once again we are back to practice rather than theory as the driver.

Key Insight 3
Realized effectiveness is what motivates people to do more.

In other words, it is not inspiring visions, moral exhortation, or mounds of irrefutable evidence that convince people to change, it is the actual experience of being more effective that spurs them to repeat and build on the behavior. People can get fantastically excited and inspired, as many did when Barack Obama was elected president of the United States in 2008. But change is only a mirage unless people actually experience the reality of improvement. If that happens, they will expect and do even more. Motivated people do get better implementation, but interestingly the reverse can be more powerful. Helping people accomplish something that they have never accomplished before *causes* motivation to increase deeply (Fullan, 2011a). Such newly found motivation is tantamount to passionate commitment that is further contagious to others.

There is often a tension between resolute leaders and the group development that we will talk about in Chapter Four. By definition, the former are determined to get on with it, and thus can become impatient with those who are hesitant to get involved. Grasping change reconciles this potential conflict because those leaders who are change savvy know that they cannot become successful without the collective commitment and ingenuity of the group. This collectivity is seen not as a nuisance but rather as a necessity. Galvanizing motivation is the essential task of the change leader.

I captured much of what it means to grasp the change process in my recent book, *Motion Leadership* (Fullan, 2010b). The resolute leader who is change savvy helps people try new things under relatively nonthreatening conditions, and listens to and learns from their reactions. He or she kick-starts the change process, often acting as the initial ignition. But the process will never go anywhere unless the leader figures out how to develop ownership within the group, and I use the word *group* advisedly because the driver of sustainability is the peer culture. Put another way, at the beginning of a given change process the leader is key to get things going, but through the processes that we will describe in this chapter all successful change eventually must revolve around collective ownership. Central leadership is still important but it fosters and relies increasingly on the peer culture to achieve deep change.

Finding Effective Motivators

Let's start with the basics: what motivates people? Daniel Pink (2009) provides us with the foundation when he identifies three sources of motivation: biological drive, extrinsic rewards (incentives and punishment), and intrinsic rewards (things that make us feel good just by doing them). Leaving aside the first as irrelevant to our purposes, let's look at the second. One example of an incentive/punishment motivator is merit or performance pay. Rewards and punishment have a place under conditions of seriously limited capacity, such as where few people have the necessary skills and often do not show up for work, as is the case with teachers in some developing countries.

But if you want substantial and continuous improvement, extrinsic motivators have limited effectiveness. Pink reports on several experiments, all of which led to the same conclusion. One involved four economists in an experiment in India in which participants were asked to do several tasks (unscrambling anagrams, tossing tennis balls at a target, and so forth). They were divided into three groups who received low, medium, and high financial rewards tied to reaching performance targets. There was no difference in the success of the low and medium groups but "in eight of the nine tasks ... examined over the three experiments, higher incentives led to *worse* performance" (Pink, p. 41, italics original). Another example: when women were invited to give blood, with one group being paid, and the other being voluntary, only 30% of the former group decided to give blood, compared with 52% of the latter. Pink observes that the rewards "crowded out the intrinsic desire to do something good" (p. 48). Extrinsic rewards, in other words, narrows the reasons for doing something and makes it unlikely that the reason for the effort is coming from inside people.

After examining evidence from several other studies, Pink summarizes the findings as the "seven deadly flaws" of using carrot-and-stick incentive systems:

1. They can extinguish intrinsic motivation.

2. They can diminish performance.

3. They can crush creativity.

4. They can crowd out good behavior.

5. They can encourage cheating, shortcuts, and unethical behavior.

6. They can become addictive.

7. They can foster short-term thinking. (Pink, p. 59)

So, we know what doesn't work. But the mere act of inviting people to engage in activities for their intrinsic satisfaction will not, by itself, do the trick either. Therefore the question becomes under what conditions will intrinsic rewards flourish. There are four core ingredients essential for intrinsic motivation to have a chance of kicking in—the first three of which are identified by Pink. For starters the work must carry with it a strong sense of *purpose*. Once their basic needs are met the vast majority of people want to do something of value. They want to do something that is meaningful. Second, people find that getting better at something that is important is intrinsically satisfying. Let's call that increased *capacity*. Third, there needs to be a degree of *autonomy* so that people can exercise judgment in making headway. The fourth element, which Pink mentions but does not highlight, is being well connected to others in the pursuit of significant goals—what we can call *camaraderie* in relation to accomplishing purpose. This collective capacity is crucial for deep and sustainable success and is the subject of Chapter Four.

These are the ingredients, but how do you realize them? This gets us back to our practitioner-driven base. To bring intrinsic satisfaction to the fore, change leaders must help create the *experiences* that turn out to be motivating because people find them emotionally meaningful relative to their values and their ability to fulfill them. It is not that the task becomes simplified but rather that it becomes directionally clear to the point that enabling the new experiences will further increase clarity, skill, and accomplishment through action. These outcomes are tantamount to the kind of ownership that comes from intrinsic motivation.

When Jamie McCracken became director of education of the Ottawa Catholic District School Board in 2003, he did exactly that. Recall that he took over a system that was "clenched," to use his word. He then set out to unleash the energy and commitment of the group. With input from the masses, he identified three core priorities: student success, staff success, and stewardship of resources. To underscore their importance, he also stated that the three goals would remain the same for all seven years of his tenure. McCracken committed, in other words, to stay the course.

But that is still just talk. To be successful McCracken had to help make these goals a real part of people's everyday experiences. So now we arrive at the real focus of this chapter: How do you galvanize motivation when you have the direction right but people are skeptical of whether it will happen—or even doubt that it is a good idea?

We get some good leads from Charles Jacobs (2010) in his *Management Rewired,* which draws essentially the same conclusions as Pink. Jacobs reinforces Pink's argument—backing it up with new research on the brain—that force, rewards, and punishment can never be lasting motivators. The only thing that can possibly work is figuring out how to activate, tap into, and leverage people's intrinsic motivation. He calls it "managing upside down."

Citing several experiments, Jacobs reports evidence that extrinsic motivation created by rewards leads to a decrease in intrinsic motivation because external rewards take away or substitute other reasons for doing something, and thus have no staying power. Telling and rewarding, in other words, have no lasting value.

Although Jacobs goes a little too far for my liking in opening up the process, the gist of his advice is very close to the mark:

> Rather than tell employees what to do and create all the negative relationship dynamics, the manager needs to ask. Rather than hand objectives to the employee the manager should ask the employee to set them. Rather than give employees feedback on their performance, the manager should ask them how they think they're doing. Rather than tell employees how to fix a problem, the manager should ask them what they should do to fix it. This of course is counterintuitive, for it turns the relationship upside down. (p. 83)

The process that Jacobs is getting at is not as aimless and random as it appears. People are turned on by doing something meaningful as long as they have a hand in identifying it. And they like to be part of a group. Therefore, suggests Jacobs, we need to "create an environment that selects for the behavior we desire" (p. 90). Put another way, we need to create the processes and conditions where frequent interaction is directed at new capacities and group identity. Increase the quality of interaction and the availability of good information and reap the benefits—look for and reinforce promising patterns.

We have developed such a process, which we call "motion leadership." It proactively shapes and trusts the "ready-fire-aim" process. Ready is directional; it identifies some core goals as priorities. But rather than forcing the ideas, motion leadership "trusts the process," knowing that an effective change leader—one who commands the seven components in this book (see Figure 1.1)—can greatly influence what happens. The process predictably generates intrinsic commitment and collective identity, both of which are powerful steering and sustaining forces. Leaders can still have (and should have) "aspirational visions," but they need to pursue them indirectly, looking for opportunities to activate and align the needs of individuals and the group. Forcing the process will be counterproductive. Engaging with it along the lines suggested in the next section will produce deeper and more lasting results.

Before delving into motion leadership let's be clear about what I am getting at. Essentially the effective change leader activates, enables, and mobilizes human and moral purpose and the skills to enact them. Here is an illustration of the kind of motivation to which I am referring. Schwartz and Sharpe (2010), in writing about "practical wisdom" (a theme that resonates with the change leader focus of my book), report on "the wise custodian."

Schwartz and Sharpe tell us about an interview with Luke, a custodian at a major teaching hospital. Luke talks about the time when he cleaned a young comatose patient's room, but the patient's father, who had been keeping a vigil for months, hadn't seen him do it, and snapped at him for not cleaning the room. So Luke did it again, graciously. When asked to explain why, here is what Luke said:

> I kind of knew the situation about his son. His son had been here for a long time and ... from what I hear, had got into a fight and he was paralyzed ... and he was in a coma and wasn't coming out of the coma.... Well ... I went and cleaned his room. His father would stay here every day, all day, but he smoked cigarettes. So, he went out to smoke ... and after I cleaned the room he came back.... I ran into him in the hall and he just freaked out ... and telling me I didn't do it ... and all this stuff. And at first, I got on the defensive, and was going to argue with him. But I don't know. Something caught me and I said, "I'm sorry, I'll go clean the room."

> [After a probe from the interviewer, Luke said], Yeah I cleaned it so he could see me clean it.... I can understand how he could be. It was like six months that his son was here. He's be a little frustrated, and so I cleaned it again. But I wasn't angry with him. I guess I could understand. (Schwarz & Sharpe, 2010, pp. 13–14)

As the authors point out, Luke's job says nothing directly about responsibility and care for patients. Luke knew that cleaning rooms was his real job, but he had figured out that another central part of his job was to make patients and their families feel comfortable, to divert them, cheer them up when they were down, and so on.

A wise person, says Schwartz and Sharpe, knows the deeper aims of what they are doing, is perceptive and can improvise, uses emotions as an ally of reason, and learns from experience.

This is the kind of learning that can't be directly taught. But change leaders can shape the conditions and processes that will "cause" it to be learned. Change leaders, or system changers, as Schwartz and Sharpe call them, "have to build institutions with the culture and organization to encourage wisdom in everyday practice. They have to create communities of practitioners who not only nurture moral skill but help inspire moral will, the commitment to do right by those the practitioners serve" (p. 272).

Thus, motion leadership causes positive movement. It creates a process and a set of conditions that foster moral will and skill, as well as technical expertise. It builds these aspects into the culture by increasing the likelihood that peers will influence peers with respect to both moral will and technical expertise. In short, motion leadership increases intrinsic motivation and identity that results in collective ownership commitment to keep going. Motion leadership generates new energy within the group to reach new heights, which is achievable because individuals, the group, and its leaders *collectively* want more, and know that it can be had.

Motion Leadership

Motion leadership is simply leadership that causes positive movement. It is especially impressive when it causes movement in situations where people are initially skeptical. Despite my characterization of management consultants in Chapter One, we find the answer in a metaphor made popular by Peters and Waterman in their book *In Search of Excellence* (1982), namely that success follows a "ready-fire-aim" sequence. In his chapter titled "Tom Peters Talks to God," Stewart (2009) quotes Peters' admission that he more or less made up the eight attributes of excellent companies by relying on his own gut perception (p. 230). So perhaps the reason I find his metaphor apt, then, is because Peters was operating from his own view of practice, not from theory.

In our own work with practitioners we have noticed nine specific insights that are congruent with the ready-fire-aim mindset (see Exhibit 3.1).

Exhibit 3.1: Ready-Fire-Aim

- Relationships first
- Beware of fat plans
- Behaviors before beliefs
- Honor the implementation dip
- Communication during implementation is paramount
- Learn about implementation during implementation
- Excitement prior to implementation is fragile
- Take risks and learn
- It is OK to be assertive

The insights boil down to the rather unexciting conclusion that if you want to be a successful change leader you have to create the conditions for people to experience the pressure and support of collective learning, and to do so in very specific, concrete ways. (The excitement comes later when you are actually accomplishing something.) Exhibit 3.2 presents the Motion Leadership Rating Form, which allows you to assess your own motion leadership skill set. The nine elements are listed down one column with a simple five-point rating scale attached to the list. After you have read about each element in the pages that follow, rate your own skill as a change leader on the characteristic in question. At the end you will total your score to get your overall rating. This information will be valuable in deciding where your strengths lie and where you should focus your efforts to grow your skills.

Relationships First

Think about the last time you were appointed to a new leadership position and you were heading for your first day on the job. These days, all newly appointed leaders, by definition, have a mandate to bring about change. The first problem the newcomer faces is the too-fast–too-slow dilemma. If the leader comes on too strong, the culture will rebel (and guess who is leaving town). If the leader is overly respectful of the existing culture, he or she will become absorbed into the status quo. What to do? Take in the following good advice from Herold and Fedor (2008). Change-savvy leadership, they say, involves

- Careful entry to the new setting
- Listening to and learning from those who have been there longer
- Engaging in fact finding and joint problem solving
- Carefully (rather than rashly) diagnosing the situation

- Forthrightly addressing people's concerns
- Being enthusiastic, genuine, and sincere about the change circumstances
- Obtaining buy-in for what needs fixing and
- Developing a credible plan for making that fix

Exhibit 3.2: Motion Leadership Rating Form

On a scale of 1 to 5 with 5 being the highest, rate your Motion Leadership on each of the nine qualities:

	(1) Weak	(2) OK	(3) Middling	(4) Strong	(5) Very Strong	Total
1. Relationships First						
2. Beware of Fat Plans						
3. Behavior Before Beliefs						
4. Implementation Dip						
5. Communication During Implementation						
6. Learn During Implementation						
7. Prior Excitement Is Fragile						
8. Take Risks and Learn						
9. Be Assertive						
*Total Score:						

*Your total score will be in the range of 9–45.
If your score is 30 or above, you are on the right track.
If below 30, you should worry.
Appreciate your strengths (the items on which you scored 5).
Work on your weaknesses (items where you scores 1 or 2).

Source: Michael Fullan, 2010.

What should strike you is not the charismatic brilliance of the new leaders but their "careful entry," "listening," and "engaging in fact finding and joint problem solving." In other words, attend to the new relationships that have to be developed. There are situations, of course, where the culture is so toxic that the leader may need to clean house. Or there might be one "derailer" who stands out, whom few like, and who requires immediate action, but by and large leaders must develop relationships first to a degree before they can push challenges. In other words, if you want to challenge people to change, develop a relationship with them first. You only get one chance to make a first impression, and it had better be a good one—not too fast, nor too slow.

Steve Munby, when he was appointed the CEO of the National College for School Leadership in England in 2005 (recently renamed National College for Leadership of Schools and Children's Services), knew about the too-fast–too-slow dilemma. The National College had lost its focus under the previous CEO, trying to be all things to all people. Steve knew that refocusing was essential. He had some ideas, but the first thing he did was make 500 phone calls to school heads across the country asking them what the college meant to them, what it could do to serve them better, and so on. One month later (it takes a while to phone 500 people and make a personal connection), he had conveyed to the country that change was coming and that he was going to listen and act. The National College went on to reestablish a strong presence in the field, helping to develop school leaders across the country and to prepare and support the next generation of school heads.

He moved fast, but not too fast, and he was careful to build relationships as he went.

Greg Mortenson learned a similar lesson in working with local leaders in northern Pakistan and Afghanistan in building schools mostly for girls (Mortenson & Relin, 2009). Although there have been questions recently about some of the details of his accomplishments, Mortenson discovered early on how important attending to building relationships was—especially in a culture that he did not understand. He spent from sunrise to sunset at the construction site of his first school. Progress was too slow for his liking, as he was forced to cope with various delays, such as workers who had other priorities. At one point the local village leader, Haji Ali, took him aside and said, "You have done much for my people and we appreciate it. But now you must do one more thing for me" (p. 149). Greg replied he'd do anything. Here was Haji's request:

> Sit down. And shut your mouth. You're making everyone crazy.... If you want to thrive in Baltistan you have to respect our ways. The first time you share tea with a Balti, you are a stranger. The second time you take tea, you are an honored guest. The third time you share a cup of tea, you become family, and for our family, we are prepared to do anything, even die.... Dr. Greg, you must take time to share three cups of tea. (p. 150)

Says Greg, "That day, Haji Ali taught me the most important lesson I've ever learned in my life ... to slow down and make building relationships as important as building projects" (p. 150).

Three weeks later, the building was finished and Greg Mortenson went on to help local villagers build 171 schools as of 2010, including 15 in Afghanistan, all in slightly more than a decade—with 9/11 smack in the middle.

Take a minute now to rate yourself on the scale of 1–5 in terms of how good you are at attending to relationships first (Exhibit 3.2).

Beware of Fat Plans

We have found that there is a natural tendency for leaders to overplan "on paper." Our colleague Doug Reeves (2009) captures it wonderfully: "The size and the prettiness of the plan is inversely related to the quality of action and the impact on student learning" (p. 81). Once you say this, it becomes obvious. Why are planning and plans so seductive? Because there are *no people* on those pages! PowerPoint slides don't talk back. Theoreticians err on the side of abstraction, often including too many elements superficially treated.

This does not mean you should skip the planning cycle. After all, there is "ready" in the ready-fire-aim trio. So, do focus on the right priorities. Do attend to relationships. But get to action sooner, and treat it as learning period. Go light on judgment at this stage. Mintzberg (2004) has it right when he observes that early planning and implementation is more like "strategizing" than it is like "strategy." Strategy is an interactive process, suggests Mintzberg, with successful ones "evolving from experience" (p. 55).

Once again, focused simplicity prevails. Time and again, Reeves has found that big, wordy plans don't move very well. In advocating making plans as simple as possible, but not more so, he concludes, "There is evidence that schools are well served by plans that are clearly focused and sufficiently simple so that all participants in the process understand their role in executing the plans" (2009, p. 83). Less is more if you know the essence of motion leadership. For example, York Region District, a large multicultural district just north of Toronto, had a 45-page improvement plan in 2007, then a 22-page plan in 2008, and by 2009 an 8-page plan. The more you know, the briefer you get. Plans still exist, but the line between written plans and action is very thin—more permeable, more two-way, and more dynamic.

Another example of going from impenetrable fat to skinny action is reported in Chapter Four where, upon our advice a superintendent of education took his 31-page plan (single-spaced with 16 goals and 8 actions for each—a grid with 128 cells), and reduced it to three goals with targeted action. With this simple change and a few sessions with us to engage school leadership teams in defining the actions, the district went from stagnation to significant improvement in student achievement within one year. The school leadership teams were doing some good things prior to our involvement, but they were stymied by a top-heavy, dense document.

Plans are only as good as the action they inspire. Thus they have to be clear, specific, communicable, "sticky," linked to action, and above all internalized by the vast majority of people. The test is whether people use the language of the plan as they do the work. If you took any ten employees at random and asked them individually to describe the organization plan—key goals and strategies—would you get a consistently clear response? Strong implementation plans are more for employees than they are for the board of directors. Speaking of boards, I am well aware that boards and governing agencies sometimes require elaborate plans. You can still meet this requirement and focus on simpler, action-oriented plans with employees. In short, send your fat plans up the hierarchy, and send your skinny ones downward where they can do some good. Good plans are more for the implementers than the planners.

Rate your company's implementation plan (Exhibit 3.2). Is it fat and forgetful, or slim and sticky?

Behavior Before Beliefs

Research on attitudinal change has long found that our behaviors change before our beliefs do. By behavior I don't mean aimless actions, but rather purposeful experiences. It is new experiences that generate feelings and emotions. The implication for approaching new change is clear. Do not load up on vision, evidence, and sense of urgency. Rather, give people new experiences in relatively nonthreatening circumstances, and build on them, especially through interaction with trusted peers. This sounds simple, but it can be hard to do when you are impatient for buy-in. This approach of course is entirely congruent with our fundamental stance that practice drives beliefs more than the reverse.

Jamie Oliver is a celebrity chef who grew up in England, established a highly successful restaurant in London called Fifteen, and became increasingly interested in helping people eat more nutritious food. As obesity was becoming more prevalent, especially among children, Jamie became more and more committed to making a difference. He knew that he could produce better food that was nutritious, tasty, and inexpensive. Seeming to have great instincts about how to lead change, he also knew that he could get nowhere by presenting the facts. Practice drives practice was the approach he took.

He started with one secondary school, named Kidbrooke. After being depressed by what the kids were eating (nutritionists and doctors at the local hospital reported huge numbers of cases of constipation in preteens, including finding unformed feces backing up into their stomachs), Oliver became even more determined to do something about it. His first challenge was Nora, the "head dinner lady" who would have no part of his fancy ways—she had over 1,000 mouths to feed, on time, and at 37 pence a stomach. He tried to work alongside Nora but couldn't do anything right according to her. The more he got inside school kitchens the more he saw that the kitchen staff were not cooks, they rather warmed up prepackaged processed food.

Partly for his own sanity ("I have to get her out of the kitchen") and partly to have Nora experience firsthand what it is like to cook properly, he arranged for her to spend a week working with his chefs at his London restaurant, Fifteen. His head chef, Arthur Potts Dawson, began to teach Nora basic knife skills in cutting vegetables, then he moved on to not overcooking, then to a rule that Nora never heard of—never send a new dish out that you haven't tasted (she did taste one of Arthur's dishes, but it was so delicious she sat down and ate the whole bowl). Gradually, these new behaviors began to make sense to Nora, and she started to alter her beliefs (but not before overcoming a dozen more change obstacles). She changed because she *experienced* new ways that turned out to be better, even though she was deeply skeptical at the beginning.

With some success at Kidbrooke, Jamie realized that changing one school had little value. He then decided to take on a whole borough. He worked out an arrangement with Greenwich, a local school district in London that had 60 schools,

20,000 students (and of course 60 head dinner ladies). The account of this journey is well portrayed in the documentary series, *Jamie's School Dinners* (Oliver, 2005).

The gist of what he did is a classic example of combining resolute purpose with impressive empathy. Instead of giving up on the head dinner ladies, he supported them in getting new experiences and skills (albeit frustrations all around in the beginning—see the next lesson, "honor the implementation dip"). Instead of giving up when students and their parents wanted no part of his recipes (they would not try them), he persisted, involved students in cooking new things, analyzing the ingredients of what they were eating, and so on. Ready-fire-aim—aspirational vision, patiently establishing new behavioral experiences, developing supportive leaders and peers, and reinforcing and consolidating gains. He used behavior as the vehicle to get at new beliefs. Within three years he had made a major positive impact on the eating habits of 20,000 kids and their families. Just so that we don't forget the humility of the change agent—success in one situation does not transfer the next one—Jamie had a harder time in affecting the eating habits of Huntington, West Virginia (which he deemed to be the "most unhealthy town in the United States"). It didn't help being a foreigner coming to save the people. Nonetheless, his success in Greenwich was impressive. He did it by using new behaviors and experiences as the route to changing basic beliefs.

Back to Exhibit 3.2. Do you appreciate in your actions that behaviors and new experiences need to precede beliefs? Do you expect people to deeply believe in the new direction before they have had the opportunity to struggle with the new behaviors, skills, and underlying beliefs?

Honor the Implementation Dip

For a long time, we have been finding that when organizations try something new, even if there has been some preimplementation preparation, the first few months are bumpy. How could it be otherwise? New skills and understandings have a learning curve. Once we brought this out in the open, a lot of people immediately felt better knowing that it is normal and everyone goes through it. This finding led to the realization that we needed to focus on capacity building at this critical stage.

Herold and Fedor (2008) have found the same phenomenon in business, and they furnish additional insights (see Figure 3.1).

Three things stand out. First is the myth of change. Those who introduce the change (usually far removed from the implementation scene) assume that there will be some immediate gains. It can't be thus—by definition. Second, look inside the "depth of decline" triangle. If you are an implementer, the costs to you are immediate and concrete, whereas the benefits

Figure 3.1: The Myth and the Reality of Change

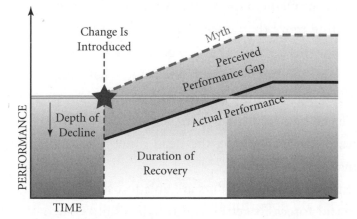

Source: Herold & Fedor, 2008.

are distant and theoretical. Thus, the cost-benefit ratio is out of whack in favor of the negative. People on balance are not having a plus day at this stage of the change process. Third, if you are a leader, here is the essence: don't expect many compliments! People are not having a good time. Leaders, therefore, have to be aware that their job is to help people get through the dip. In effect, change-savvy leadership works to increase the upward slope of the bottom line of the triangle (decreasing the duration of recovery) so that the breakthrough in the time line to the plus side occurs sooner, that is, it crosses the plane sooner from the negative to the positive zone. In our best efforts this positive development occurs within six months. When the breakthrough occurs, a blast of new energy is unleashed, as people are palpably motivated by the fact that they are getting somewhere.

Change leaders with deep moral purpose learn to overcome the inevitable first barriers. Jamie Oliver, starting into what looked like a straightforward problem (get kids to eat good-tasting food that is infinitely better for them), quickly stumbled into the implementation dip. And, he stayed there a while, lamenting more than once, "God, I feel so uninspired. I can't work like this because I have to be inspired to work. I am so far out of my comfort zone with respect to what I normally cook. I am getting so grumpy. I am confused and harassed" (2005). Jamie had natural change savvy, and found other ways to move forward, such as getting the head dinner ladies on board as change agents.

Effective change leaders are able to use a small number of powerful forces to get breakthrough results—such as having immense moral commitment to a cause along with empathy for those they are dealing with. This combination of resolute leadership and empathy enables these leaders to find alternative approaches when they get stuck. They engage implementers in figuring out the actions, activating or linking behavior to intrinsic goals, and using peers to influence peers. They demonstrate persistence with flexibility but never stray from the core purpose, displaying the resolute leadership we examined in the previous chapter.

Now rate yourself on your capacity to "honor the implementation dip" in change initiatives that you lead (Exhibit 3.2).

Communication During Implementation Is Paramount

Put directly, communication during implementation is far more important than communication prior to implementation. Wendy Thomson, as new CEO of a borough in England, spent a year talking up the vision in all quarters of the organization only to discover that, at best, 4% favored the new direction. She is an articulate and engaging person. How can spending a whole year with the community and staff discussing an exciting new future yield such a paltry buy-in? The answer is that communication in the abstract, in the absence of action, means almost nothing. It means a little but not much because without action words have no grounded substance—nothing to stir your emotions. Leaders must increase the quality of two-way communication *during* implementation if they are to be successful.

Once you start action—"fire" in Peters' language—communication means something concrete, for better or worse. The change leader accomplishes several critical things at this stage. First, problems get identified through constant two-way communication. Information is based on specific occurrences. Second, the leader has multiple opportunities to communicate and refine the vision in relation to concrete implementation and—this is crucial—to state the essence of the implementation strategy itself. In short, problems get solved, a "we" (rather than "us-them") identity around a common vision gets strengthened, and people come to know the implementation strategy.

Ontario's Dalton McGuinty exemplifies this principle. Despite being the province's premier, with a host of other demanding responsibilities, McGuinty always stays close to the action. For instance, as part of a project called Leader to Leader, he meets four times a year with a group of 20 school principals (10 from difficult schools that have had success, and 10 from schools that are still struggling). The discussion is focused on what it is like to be a leader in tough times; what he faces, for example, in the financial recession with its crushing priorities, what the school principals are dealing with, what's working, and what are the most difficult problems at hand.

McGuinty creates and responds to every opportunity he can because, as he said in a recent speech to a group of state leaders in Washington, D.C., the first lesson is that "the drive to make progress cannot be a fad." You have to stay the course on the ground. McGuinty knows that you have to communicate and listen every day during implementation. He takes his core compass of the small number of priorities (literacy, numeracy, high school graduation), and the essence of his motion leadership strategy (capacity building with a focus on results going light on judgment) wherever he goes.

The masses know what he stands for because he walks the talk day after day.

We also saw the value of persistence and on-the-spot communication in Isadore Sharp's shaping of the Four Seasons brand. He constantly visited his hotels around the world, always restating the core aims, asking how it was going, and talking just as much to frontline employees as to mangers. Then in his hiring and cultivation of leaders, he strove to have leaders who modeled this two-way communication in everything they did. Consistent communication during implementation is essential to getting the collective clarity and energy necessary for success. Communication sticks best when it is close to action in time and place and is frequently reinforced.

Rate this one carefully on Exhibit 3.2. Do you really do the small stuff of frequent communication, or do you do what most leaders do—communicate just on the big occasions?

Learn About Implementation During Implementation

One of the most powerful strategies we have employed is to find different ways for implementers to learn from other implementers, especially those in similar circumstances who are further down the line. Leaders learn how to build collaborative cultures within their organizations and to look for ways where units or branches can learn from each other. One strategy that we use in school system reform is the Schools on the Move initiative in Toronto, in which some 145 schools that have had three successive years of improvement in literacy and numeracy have been identified, examined as to how they did it, and then given resources to help other schools in similar circumstances.

This is not a "why can't you be more like your brother" strategy but rather a recognition that this is very hard work, some are figuring it out, and we can learn from them. Effective leaders realize that many of the answers are out there, in pockets, and that one powerful strategy is to draw on and spread the wisdom of crowds. We will return to this matter with more examples in Chapter Four, when we examine the impact of focused collaboration. We will also see that extended, more loosely connected networks are essential in order to prime innovation. Once you start to implement innovations, the best, most effective learning is characterized by precision, specificity, targeted feedback, new experiences that spark your intrinsic interests, and the added opportunity to learn from peers who are farther down the path. The key to motivating the masses is to make the peer culture the driver.

On Exhibit 3.2—rate how you are doing at unleashing the potential of the peers to learn from each other during implementation.

Excitement Prior to Implementation Is Fragile

If your anticipation is greater than your fulfillment, then you are not very good at implementation. Excitement in advance of doing something is understandable, but it does not have much of a foundation. Indeed, the fall into the implementation dip will be even greater if high aspirations precede it. Premature excitement is no substitute for the hard work of implementation. Everything we know about motivation tells us that deep excitement comes from doing something worthwhile, doing it well, and getting results. You can't do this during planning or vision sessions (or if you do generate enthusiasm it is bound to be superficial). You have to earn and experience excitement. You can't fake it.

Thus, knowledgeable change leaders strive for small early successes, acknowledge real problems, admit mistakes, protect their people, and celebrate success along the way. They love genuine results that generate great pride in the organization. They have their finger on the energy pulse of people, knowing that it will ebb and flow but will be spurred by positive results.

Excitement during implementation when it occurs is solidly based on substance. York Region, for example, holds an annual Learning Fair in which every one of its 190 schools prepares a 25-minute multimedia presentation. They present what they set out to accomplish at the beginning of the year, what measurable results they obtained, strategies used, obstacles encountered, lessons learned, and so on. Talk about excitement! The room is abuzz with emotion. As one participant says, "It is days like this that I wish were 36 hours long." People cannot get enough. It is real and spontaneous because it is about what is actually being done. If you ask participants to describe the Learning Fair in one word the most frequent utterance is "energizing."

The notion that people become energized *as a result of accomplishing something* is turning out to be an absolutely crucial breakthrough in our change work because it is a phenomenon in which previously stagnant people literally *change* for the better. I call it the transformative power of "realization." To take a recent example from our work in improving the Ontario school system with its 4,900 schools and 2 million students, consider the following account.

One of the strategies we use is called the "critical learning pathway." It consists of a six-week cycle whereby teachers bring samples of their students' writing so that they can be helped in assessing the quality of the writing according to a set of standards, and in turn to use some targeted instructional strategies to help their students improve. They go back and forth over the six weeks, helped by a facilitator. In the debriefing at the end of one such cycle, a veteran grade 4 teacher who had taught for over 25 years came to the microphone in tears and said:

> I came to these Professional Development sessions because my principal sent me, saying she needed some staff to attend. At the first session I knew that I should not have come. I looked at samples of grade 4 writing from other teachers and I felt really badly—I had been teaching for years and knew that my students could never produce such high-quality writing. I did my best though to follow the process, feeling sick at heart for my kids.
>
> But as the cycle progressed my classroom soared. [Here the tears flowed in earnest.] Every one of my kids produced writing at the high end of the standard—some at the top level. They all doubled or tripled the gains that I had predicted. I realized that for 25 years of teaching, I have set my goals too low. How many more of my students could have reached so much higher if only I had known I could take them there? (in Fullan, 2011a, p. 20)

This is excitement during implementation—undeniably powerful. No amount of public rallying in advance of implementation would have excited this teacher. And for any teacher who would be inspired by advanced hype it would have been fragile because there is no excitement that can match the real McCoy of accomplishment. Experiencing success like never before proves it can be done, stirs the emotions, and energizes us. There is nothing stronger than the intrinsic motivation that comes from being successful at something that has deep meaning for you.

Now, rate your leadership on the 1–5 scale according to how much you rely on hyped motivation as distinct from the motivation that derives from the harder work of actual accomplishment (Exhibit 3.2).

Take Risks and Learn

Back to Jamie McCracken, the director of the Ottawa Catholic District School Board. In addition to reducing the number of priorities, McCracken made it clear that people should try new things and learn from their experiences. Risk taking as learning became the district's modus operandi. There was a license to innovate and problem solve. Today, Ottawa has become a high-performing district in literacy, numeracy, high school graduation, and is valued as a great place to work. People are engaged, energized, and collectively committed to continuous improvement.

The critical importance and role of risk taking is known by all organizations that are consistently successful. Ready-fire-aim represents purposeful learning, and taking learning risks is embedded in the psyche of successful organizations. To take risks and learn you really have to have the growth mindset that Dweck uncovered. You take risks *in order to learn*. This means that you have to foster a culture and atmosphere of non-judgmentalism. One of the biggest barriers to improvement in school systems is the presence of punitive accountability. If you fail you will be put on a watch list. We have already seen that punishment (and even its opposite, reward) can never lead to intrinsic motivation to put in the effort to solve a problem and to sustain one's interest in solving inevitable future problems. Nonjudgmentalism is the ability to perceive a problem without being pejorative or negative about it (Fullan, 2008). Without this stance problems will be kept hidden or will be distorted—it's not my fault. A growth mindset, combined with nonjudgmentalism wrapped in transparency and open sharing, actually produces almost all the accountability you need. So leaders need to model risk taking, nonjudgmentalism, and learning from mistakes, and foster all these in others.

On the scale of 1–5, how good are you at modeling and fostering nonjudgmental risk taking and learning in your organization?

It's OK to Be Assertive

Many of the potentially best leaders in these democratic times are often reticent to assert themselves. To know about change is to know about inertia, which is to say that sometimes the status quo needs a wake-up call. You can't wait for change to happen; you have to kick-start it. Leadership is a mixture of authority and democracy. Leaders can get away with being assertive under three conditions: (1) when they have built trusted relationships, (2) when it turns out they have a good idea, and (3) when they empower people from day one to help assess and shape the idea.

Do you think Jamie Oliver was holding back when he said, "This food is crap. I wouldn't serve it to my dog"? ("Well actually I would serve it to my dog," he added.) Did Dalton McGuinty conduct a series of consultative meetings when he was elected in 2003 on whether literacy, numeracy, and high school graduation rates would be his government's core priorities? No, these leaders just went ahead and acted, using their change knowledge to empower people and problem solve as they went. These leaders do not go around making random assertions. They learn first and always as they go. There is definitely a tension with our reference to Jacobs' "managing upside down," but I am saying that it is OK to be assertive when you know enough to identify a promising direction, and you then create many opportunities for people to assess, shape, and decide on its worth.

One the matter of having good ideas, effective leaders *participate as learners* in helping the organization move forward. Participate as a learner for a few years and guess what? You really do come to have good ideas.

Make your final entry on the Motion Leadership Rating Form—what is your "Be Assertive" rating on the 1–5 scale? Now, total the scores on the chart and review your overall score (30+ is strong), and your profile of strengths and weaknesses. Finish up by writing a "note to self" committing to actions you will take to reinforce your strong attributes, and map out a brief plan of action to tackle one or two of your weak points.

Really Motivating the Masses

As we have seen, galvanizing motivation is strongly practice based, not theory based. The theory comes later after you have understood why and how it works in practice. The flow goes something like this:

1. To get anywhere, you have to *do* something. Give people the experience and build on it.

2. In doing something, you need to focus on developing *skills*.

3. Acquisition of skills increases *clarity*.

4. New experiences, skills, and clarity stirs *intrinsic motivation*, if the idea is a good one.

5. Intrinsically meaningful experiences equals *ownership*.

6. Doing this together with others generates *shared ownership*.

7. *Persist* no matter what, being flexible as you learn more.

Now you see why ready-fire-aim is the correct sequence. Focused meaning is the result. Effective leaders do have ideas to begin with, but they then must balance persistence with learning more. They grasp change as the process of uncovering new and better practices that must mobilize the whole group. None of this is mechanical. It requires a light touch. Leaders must learn to become change savvy by reflective doing. It's messy at first, but you eventually get somewhere, and get good at doing it. It works because the group develops capacity and begins to believe in themselves as they see the results. They experience and feel the success. The key insight again: the critical motivator is *realized* effectiveness. The emotional experience of doing and accomplishing something worthwhile with others sticks with you.

Motivating vast numbers in the organization requires understanding the sequence of mobilization. In situations of stagnation or terrible performance, leadership has to be the driver at the outset. This is not about being assertive concerning the content but rather being proactive with respect to all nine elements of the ready-fire-aim phenomenon. In other words, strong, high-initiative leadership is crucial at the beginning of a change process.

Second, if you are going to reach large numbers, and if there is going to be any chance of building in sustainability, you have to reach and empower peers. In all large-scale examples of success that I know of, such as the eight sites we recently filmed, the process was assertively led at the beginning (the process, not the content of change). And in every case after some solid success had been achieved, when leaders were asked what would happen if you left, the instant response was, "I am now less important because the peer culture is the driver" (Fullan, 2010c).

The same finding comes out of the McKinsey & Co. study of the 20 school systems that keep improving (Mourshed, Chinezi, & Barber, 2010). If capacity is very low to begin with, you need to have more focus and requirements; as capacity develops (including the capacity to collaborate) the peer culture drives innovation and further improvement. Leadership is still key, but it is in the service of the peer culture. Prescribe adequacy, unleash greatness, the study concludes. When capacity is high, the focus is on stressing peer-based learning, and "system sponsored innovation and experimentation" (p. 26). It is at this stage that you can really reach the masses because lots of peers are engaged in influencing each other and are enabled in doing so by central strategies designed to support and spread such learning.

Stated differently, hierarchical leadership, no matter how good, can never reach the masses, but purposeful peers can. As Pascale, Sternin, and Sternin (2010) say, "Key to lasting networks is finding ways to help others be more successful" (p. 185). To unleash the peers is not to give up control, quite the contrary. Peers working toward important moral purpose goals, because they interact openly with each other and with data, and because they are enabled to do so by the hierarchy, have a built-in capacity to innovate and cohere as they sift through what is working and what is not. Motivating the masses is tantamount to building the social capital of the group in action.

Also encouraging is that with the right ingredients mobilizing the masses becomes predictable even when no one seems to be in charge. Peter Miller (2010) calls this phenomenon *the smart swarm*. He examines how this happens with ants, honeybees, termites, sparrows, and locusts. Miller shows time and again that smart swarms occur spontaneously under three conditions: *"decentralized control, distributed problem solving, and multiple interactions"* (p. 10). Solutions to problems occur as multiple interactions generate best solutions, which are retained because they work. We see that "friendly competition" (I call this *collaborative competition* in Chapter Four) is better at addressing complex problems. Again though, the conditions are important here: decentralized control and distributed problem solving are necessary antidotes to failing to consider alternative solutions, or to succumbing to groupthink.

The subtitle to Miller's book is *How Understanding Flocks, Schools, and Colonies Can Make Us Better at Communicating, Decision Making, and Getting Things Done.* But how can bugs, birds, and bees be like humans? They aren't, of course—they lack deliberate self-will, to name one nontrivial difference. Yet, the conditions and processes in smart swarms generate the same patterns in human interaction. We are not talking about an analogy or metaphor here—*it is the same phenomenon at work!*

We have known for some time now from "complexity theory" that when you combine quality of information with quality interaction, and then look for and extract promising patterns, you get new ideas that are by definition shared by the group (Wheatley, 2006). The "attractors" (pattern makers) here, to use a term from complexity science, that cause regular convergence are mutual allegiance, shared values, and evidence-based success that fuels additional energy, especially on the part of the group. The greater the capacity of the group, the more you can rely on the peer culture to be the driver—as long as you are an engaged leader. The lesson for leaders is *be engaged and trust the process.* It is as reliable as the birds and bees at work.

In short, change leaders know that they need to use their resolution and grasp of the change process not just to help individuals cope, but also to mobilize the power of the collectivity. There are few things more powerful than the commitment of the group. Change leaders need the group to change the group: when it comes to socialization there is no better teacher than one's peers. The beauty of this is that once you establish the conditions we have been discussing, peer-to-peer learning becomes built into the process, happening naturally. The effective leader uses this knowledge to advantage. We examine this powerful phenomenon up close in Chapter Four.

CHAPTER·FOUR

Collaborate to Compete

Multiply Capacity and Win

There is more to collaboration than just collaboration. Nicholas Christakis and James Fowler (2009) show us the mysterious and "surprising power of our social networks." We are hardwired, they say, "to influence and copy one another" (p. 22). Emotions and ideas are contagious. If my friend is thin, and has thin friends, I am more likely to be thin, or as they put it, "your friends' friends can make you fat" (p. 105). Certain behaviors by virtue of the fact that they exist can legitimize themselves and spread consciously and subconsciously. Christakis and Fowler quote Eric Hoffer: "When people are free to do as they please, they usually imitate each other" (p. 112).

Of course, collaboration can be good or bad (recall the World War II definition of *collaborators:* cooperating treacherously with the enemy). It is bad to be disconnected (isolation is unhealthy), misconnected (hanging around a bad group), or hyperconnected (multitaskers are superficial at many things). However, in general, more connections within a group, say Christakis and Fowler, "can reinforce a behavior in the group, but more connection between groups ... can open up a group to new behaviors" (2009, p. 117). For our purposes, we want to exploit this trait to make it easier for people to learn important new ideas and productive processes from each other. The key insight then concerns opening up the group to new ideas and friendly competition.

Key Insight 4

Collaborative competition is the yin and yang of successful change. Collaborate and compete.

Let's not romanticize group work—it is not always a good thing. Although it is true that almost all creative breakthroughs result from a combination of individual effort and teamwork, not all group work produces genius. We must always bear in mind that it is the whole model of the change leader—all seven components in Figure 1.1—operating in concert that results in ongoing success. Thus, we cannot treat collaboration in isolation from the rest of Figure 1.1. Morten Hansen's advice (2009) should be heeded:

> Bad collaboration is worse than no collaboration. People scuttle from meeting to meeting to coordinate work and share ideas but far too little gets done .... This is a terrible way of working in the best of times: resources are wasted while better players pull away. It's downright reckless in tough times, such as in a crisis, where the ability to pull together can make the difference between making it or not. (p. 1)

There are many insightful cautions in Hansen's treatment of collaboration, and though we should worry about ineffective and wasteful forms of collaboration, for our purposes we need to realize that social engagement in the service of something important is the sine qua non of effective organizations. So what does good collaboration look like?

Building Collaborative Cultures

From our own work and in examining the best examples, I have derived five elements of leading collaborative cultures that can be used to consider what might be needed (see Exhibit 4.1).

Exhibit 4.1: Elements of a Collaborative Culture

1. Focus: Set a small number of core goals.
2. Form a guiding coalition.
3. Aim for collective capacity building.
4. Work on individual capacity building.
5. Reap the benefits of collaborative competition.

Chip and Dan Heath (2010) say that one of the biggest barriers to change is the confusion and exhaustion that arises from the sheer number and complexity of goals being pursued simultaneously. "What looks like resistance," they say, "is often lack of clarity" (p. 15). The idea of element 1, then, is not to have simple goals but to have a few core ones that can be deeply pursued. It is not that those few goals will be crystal clear at the outset, but rather that they can be pursued with focus, thereby becoming clearer and better able to be implemented well.

We can use the Mayo Clinic and its century of success to illustrate. Focus should capture both the main goal(s) and the strategy to get there. For Mayo Clinic it is "preserving a patient-first legacy" by "practicing team medicine"—fewer than 10 words (Berry & Seltman, 2008). (Recall Jamie McCracken of Ottawa whose core mission consisted of seven words: "student success, staff success, stewardship of resources.")

The second element, having a guiding coalition, is also critical. The leader at the top and the key leaders at the center of the coalition must be in agreement about the core goals and strategy and be able to clearly and consistently communicate those goals. Having a strong central team means that progress does not depend on one leader. Typically this serves two purposes. One concerns communication, including listening; the second involves problem solving. The Mayo Clinic has employed this strategy consistently through 11 CEOs and generations of physicians and patients.

The third element, focus on collective capacity building, "democratizes" the change process by extending power to other members of the organization. In other words, team-based capacity building extends the core values and strategy while the latter get shaped and reshaped. This requires teamwork. For example, in the Mayo Clinic "teamwork" is not optional—it is mandatory (Berry & Seltman, 2008, p. 51). On-the-job learning from practice creates a learning laboratory:

> The combination of an integrated medical practice (in which multiple clinicians may care for one patient), an integrated medical record (in which these clinicians all use the same set of patient records), and the regulation of Mayo Clinic create strong peer pressure to practice quality

medicine. A doctor's skills and knowledge are continually on display. Internally—the peer pressure to keep learning—or leave—is real. (Berry & Seltman, 2008, p. 61)

"Collaboration, cooperation and coordination are the three dynamics that support the practice of team medicine at Mayo Clinic," observe Berry and Seltman (p. 65). Collective capacity focuses on how the team and the group function. Individual capacity is furthered through the hiring and orientation practices, learning on the job, and by functioning as a team member (learning from team leaders and peers).

The outcome, as we have seen time and again in our own work, is that purposeful collaboration continuously contributes two interrelated powerful change forces—*knowledge* of ideas and practices, and *identity* or allegiance to one's peers and the organization. As Berry and Seltman put it, "Mayo's collaborative culture fosters personal growth ... [and the success of the Clinic depends on] the continuing interest by each staff member in the professional progress of every other member" (p. 257). Higher purpose, mutual respect, high expectations, pressure and support to perform and innovate to get better make a powerful, focused collaborative culture.

We saw earlier how Gittell's framework (2009) of "relational coordination" that she applied to the health care sector leads to the same conclusions. As she found, those organizations that are dramatically more successful develop cultures of relational coordination (shared goals, shared knowledge, and mutual respect), and transparent communication (frequent, timely, accurate, and problem-solving communication). These cultures continually clarify and reinforce the focused efforts of the organization. Coordinated, focused organizations are both more efficient and more effective. The reason is that vastly more members of the organization are knowledgeable, skilled, and committed to getting things done, individually and collectively. Because core ideas are pursued collectively, day after day, they generate deeper, consistent practices across the organization. Shared depth of understanding and corresponding skills are the result.

You don't get shared depth by going to courses or workshops or by toiling away at your job individually. The organizations that are successful are focused, have consistent leadership at the center, invest in frontline leadership and peer-based learning, use data to confirm success and make corrections (see Chapter Six). They select for talent and teamwork and then cultivate the group, emphasizing learning and problem solving, not finger pointing and blame. Revealingly, organizations high on relational coordination respond to great external pressure by "engaging in higher rather than lower levels of relational coordination" (Gittell, 2009, p. 226). They have greater social cohesion and ingenuity and are thus more resilient when faced with stressful conditions.

It is worth restating that the goal of having a collaborative culture is not that employees will do the work for a resolute leader, but rather that they become *collectively* engaged in work that is also in meaningful to them. Mintzberg (2009) puts it best: "Managing seems to work especially well when it helps to bring out the energy that exists naturally within people" (p. 214). In effect, what gets created is collective leadership with those at the top directing and framing while they too are engaged in the learning enterprise.

The fourth element, individual capacity building, includes personnel decisions. Successful organizations do invest in the careful hiring and development of individuals on the job. Most employees are motivated if they experience employers who contribute to their own development on the job. One aspect of effective development is working with peers who are similarly committed to learning. Thus, effective organizations pay careful attention to whom they hire, with an eye to how individuals will work together. It may seem obvious, but collaborative cultures rarely select newcomers only on the basis of their *personal* track records. Rather, they hire largely for the person's ability to work with and lead others. Mike McCue of Tellme Networks captures it well:

> [We want people] who know they can get better; they want to learn from the best. We look for people who light up when they are around other talented people. (in Taylor & LaBarre, 2006, p. 203)

All the best collaborative cultures do this. The Mayo Clinic and Four Seasons Hotels, for example, look for "connectors" rather than lone operators when they recruit. As we have seen, Isadore Sharp of Four Seasons looks more for attitude than experience. These leaders like to start with good people who have the capacity to become better and better.

The explorer Ernest Shackleton exemplified these leadership qualities. Morrell and Capparell (2001) describe how Shackleton went about hiring his crew from "your No. 2 is your most important hire" (pick someone who complements your style), through "hire those with the talents and experiences you lack" (don't feel threatened by them), to "help your staff do top-notch work, giving them the best equipment you can afford" (don't be distracted by outdated equipment) (p. 75).

Shackleton then set about "forging a united and loyal team" (not only loyal to him but also to each other). Morrell and Capparell note his main qualities in this respect: "Take time to observe before acting; always keep the door open to staff; have people work together on certain tasks; lead by example by helping with the work; and have regular gatherings" (p. 100). The outcome was a highly talented team that endured and solved incredible problems under the most severe conditions, resulting in the healthy survival of all men despite being cut off and stranded on ice floes for almost two years.

The fifth element is masterful in its elegance and one that we discovered by accident: "collaborative competition." Collaboration is essential for success, for the reasons just stated, but we worried about whether it maximized achievement for the system. It turns out that if you put in place the conditions I am advocating in this book, competition enters naturally and, I would say, inevitably. Remember the conditions: a very important goal; resolute leadership; empathy; a ready-fire-aim press to get things done; learning from the best in each other; and transparent data about how well you and others are doing. When these conditions are in place, people push each other and try to outdo each other.

This phenomenon is shown quite clearly in Alan Boyle's study (2009) of Tower Hamlets, a very poor school district in east London. Despite high poverty, a constant stream of non-English-speaking poor immigrants, and one of the highest unemployment rates in England, Tower Hamlets outdid the rest of the country with respect to improved student achievement.

In 1997 the proficiency rates of 11-year-olds in literacy and numeracy in Tower Hamlets was 35%, compared with the national average of 58%. By 2009 they were in a dead heat with the national average, both at 80%. They did this through a lot of the strategies we have seen in this book—focus, capacity building, staying the course, collaboration, and the like. What Boyle observed was that working together on a crucial goal developed a strong sense of mutual allegiance across school leadership teams as the schools collaborated and between schools and the district leadership.

Boyle also found that once people saw the big picture and were engaged in the task that leaders and staff displayed "the mental characteristics of confidence, determination and competition to achieve success" (2009, p. 21). Thus, schools begin to compete with themselves (we can do better than last year), and with each other (if they can do it, why can't we?). Mutual allegiance comes from a commitment to the cause, and people get satisfaction from trying to outdo each other for the common good (and individual pride) even to the point of sharing ideas in a catch-me-if-you-can spirit. It is magical. You can have an Olympian spirit without cheating or cutthroat win-lose mentalities. The effective change leader appreciates both collaboration and competition all the more when it is woven into the same phenomenon. For ongoing success you need to collaborate *and* compete.

This conclusion, I think, casts new light on how successful teams work. Teamwork has become a business cliché and in the process has lost that aspect of the sports analogy that includes internal competition. A good basketball, football, or cricket team works together, but the members also compete with each other. The effects are not always good but they are necessary for high performance. The power of teamwork is captured in Ray McLean's study (2010) of successful sports teams in Australia. Team members hold themselves and each other accountable. Direct feedback from coaches is seen as essential even though it hurts sometimes. In this team-based competitive atmosphere, teams bond but also put a premium on performance. The same is true for all successful organizations. The change leader helps build a culture of mutual allegiance and healthy competition. If people become intrinsically motivated, competition to do their best comes naturally.

The nature and importance of creative collaboration is brought into dramatic historical relief in Johnson's sweeping historical examination, *Where Good Ideas Come From* (2010). His conclusion stated up front is this: "The long-zoom approach lets us see that openness and connectivity may, in the end, be more valuable to innovation than purely competitive mechanisms" (p. 21). Johnson shows that many innovative ideas derive from what he calls (borrowing from the complexity scientist Stuart Kaufmann) "the adjacent possible."

The dynamic world is full of adjacent possible opportunities, but leaders must put themselves and their organizations in a position to experience potential new ideas. Some of these are within the organization, which is why we build our work on increasing purposeful collaborative cultures within organizations. Other possibilities are "out there," which is why we foster wide-ranging connections that are not narrowly purposeful. In other words, they are exploratory and you cannot predict which connections will pay off, but you can be sure that some new ideas will arise. In short, increase your interaction with "the adjacent possible" if you want to learn more.

Organizations do need to do their focused, precise work (again, collaboratively) as I have said, but they also need to invest in some degree of exploration. Johnson cites a study of Stanford business graduates who went into entrepreneurial careers and found that "the most creative individuals had broad social networks that extended outside their organizations and involved people from diverse fields of expertise . . . [and diverse, horizontal networks] . . . were *three times* more innovative than uniform vertical networks" (Johnson, 2010, p. 166, italics in original).

In a remarkable chapter called "The Fourth Quadrant," Johnson lines up a chronology of key historical innovations from 1400 to 2000. He classifies these innovations according to whether they were individually discovered or collectively found and promoted. He further subdivides innovations as to whether they are market driven or not. Collective, non-market-generated innovations (open source collaborative networks) was the fourth quadrant. Early period innovations (1400 to 1600, and 1600 to 1800) were clustered in the individual non-market category (because networking was limited). By contrast, innovations in the later period (1800 to 2000) were heavily clustered in the non-market/networked quadrant. The reason? The opportunity for networking was widespread compared with earlier periods in history.

Dispelling two myths, Johnson concludes that (1) most innovations are not developed by solo geniuses, (2) nor are they developed in closed, private networks. Good ideas may not want to be free, says Johnson, but they do want "to connect, fuse, recombine" (p. 22).

It sounds complicated, but our simplicity rule is foster collaboration within the organization and allow room for more diffuse exploration outside the organization. You never know what unusual idea you will end up cobbling together. To paraphrase Johnson, chance favors the connected organization.

There are grander forms of collaboration that are emerging that are fundamentally congruent with the change leader as sustainable force. Ever since Peter Senge (1990) proposed that we needed sustainable, systemic solutions we have experienced a slow realization that short-term solutions are self-defeating. Collaborate to compete includes win-win partnerships. Senge's solution is now taking a more practical format in new approaches to collaboration (for example, Partnership Brokering Project; www.partnershipbrokers.org).

Partnership is one of those words that is often overused and for which there seems rarely to be an agreed definition. In education today there is a growing trend to look toward partnerships—particularly public-private partnerships—as a way to extend resources (Greg Butler, personal communication, April 14, 2011; Tennyson, 2003). New partnerships that we and others (Peter Senge, Michael Barber, Ken Robinson) are working on involve an *ongoing commitment* to work together where there are *shared benefits and risks.* In these cases projects and activities are *co-created with tangible commitments and mutual accountability.* Risk and benefits are distributed with a sense of equity and joint success. This new form of partnership and collaboration represents the sustainable future that Senge had in mind in *The Fifth Discipline,* and now appears more possible, and definitely more desperately needed. These new developments are a natural for the change leader.

Action Implications

On a small scale we saw a great practical example of collaborative development and its payoff recently in our work with an eastern Ontario school district. Their success in a relatively short time seemed effortless—or at least natural—given the right conditions, that is, the conditions we are identifying in this book. The Catholic District School Board of Eastern Ontario (CDSBEO), just outside Ottawa, has 32 elementary schools and 10 secondary schools (in Ontario, dating back to the constitution, all Catholic schools are fully funded, that is, they are wholly part of the public school system). When the director of education, Bill Gartland, approached us to help them in October 2009, he talked about their frustrations in failing to move forward despite a great deal of effort. We agreed to work with him, and asked that he send us their Board Improvement Plan for Student Achievement.

However, once we took a look at the plan our worry barometer went way up. The plan was 31 pages long, contained 16 goals ("to develop resources and support initiatives which will support justice, peace and wise use of resources; an increase from 65% to 75% grade three reading proficiency"; and 14 other goals), and 8 tasks related to each goal ("needs assessment, targeted evidence-based strategies, resources needed, leadership, monitoring" and the like) (Catholic District School Board of Eastern Ontario, 2009). In sum, there were 128 cells to be filled out—talk about fat plans!

I sent Bill Gartland an e-mail in October 2009 that said simply, "We went over the plan. Right ingredients but too long—overwhelming." To be fair, as we will see below, it is not just having a more focused plan that counts but also one's skill at execution—at leading change, in other words. As in most places, a lot of very good work was going on in the 42 schools. They had the skills to be successful but did not have a system to bring them into sustained focus. They simply had no strategy to harness and leverage the good work that was ongoing, and a dense plan was not going to help.

My colleague Lyn Sharratt and I set up four "capacity-building sessions" with the central team of the district and with school teams from the schools. At the central level they modified the plan and came up with "three stepping stones—achieving literacy for all, living our Catholic faith, and making resources matter" (Catholic District School Board of Eastern Ontario, 2010). Now, the Strategic Plan 2010–2013 could be expressed on one page in big letters! School teams who were helped by central district consultants, and lightly by us (only four sessions), zeroed in on literacy and shared ideas (central district to school, school to school). It was the internal leadership of the district at the central and school levels that made the difference; all we had to do was help them focus on the small number of right things—simplexity at its finest.

In the 2010 provincial results, less than a year later, the district had its first increase in achievement in over five years. From 2009 to 2010 the district had increased 5% or more in most of the six areas of assessment (reading, writing, and math in grade 3, and reading, writing, and math in grade 6). More than that, on November 26, 2010, we sat in on their Learning Fair, where all 42 schools shared their stories and accomplishments (published in a local resource book called *Realization*). The day was truly astonishing. Principal after principal and teacher after teacher, using multimedia resources, described what they did. The clarity and precision of what they did, how they did it, and with what impact came tripping off their tongues. The pride and mutual allegiance was palpable. The friendly competition was everywhere—we can do better than we did last year, we are just getting started, we can do better than you, and so on. It was a kind of moral Olympics of stretched accomplishments.

I was bowled over with what they had done, and I am not one to exaggerate. Clearly, they must have been at a tipping point. We did very little. It just took a tweak from us, responsiveness from district leaders, and a set of strategies that "unleashed greatness." This was all done in 13 months. And now they are energized to do much more. Realization is sustainability's driver.

One lesson here, going back to our Chapter Three treatment of "fat plans," is that effective plans are more for implementers than for central leaders. Effective plans are actionable, sticky (everyone can cite them), and practically inspiring. They point to what should be done, and engage implementers in helping the plan come alive. When we first looked at the CDSBEO plan we could easily surmise that there was no way that the 42 school principals let alone teachers would know what was in the plan—128 cells of information could never be grasped as a basis for action.

To return to Exhibit 4.1, a relatively complete example of the five elements can be found in Ontario's education reform strategy that I introduced in Chapter Two. We certainly have resolute leadership in the form of Premier Dalton McGuinty. We have a small number of core goals: literacy, numeracy, high school graduation, and lately we have added preschool learning. The guiding coalition is alive and well at the center: McGuinty, the minister of education, the deputy minister (highest ranking civil servant), myself as special adviser, and related policy associates. We meet every six weeks and have numerous small-group conversations focusing on consistency of message, monitoring progress, and taking appropriate corrective action.

Collective capacity is both political and technical. The political dimension involves forums for debate and communication, such as "working tables" that consist of stakeholders and government leaders engaged in the give-and-take discussion of goals and strategies. Technical matters focus on strategies to develop the capacity of schools, districts, and networks to improve pedagogical and collaborative competencies about literacy, numeracy, high school innovation, and early learning practices. All of this is done in a spirit of mutual respect, nonjudgmentalism, and a determination to press for results that have their own forms of pressure and support. Individual capacity building occurs within collaborative endeavors and through teacher education and leadership development.

These activities are focused on effective practices, impact on results, and learning how to become more effective. There is competition between schools within a district and among school districts, and there is an overall sense that we are competing internationally with countries around the world. And there is widespread sharing of ideas with the competition, so to speak. It pays off. McKinsey & Co. (Mourshed, Chinezi, & Barber, 2010) assessed Ontario to be one of the top five school systems in the world. The Organisation for Economic Co-operation and Development's (OECD) 2009 PISA results (Programme for International Student Assessment) found Ontario to be among the top six performers in the world in reading—along with newcomer Shanghai and other historical front-runners such as Singapore, Finland, and Hong Kong (OECD, 2010).

Once capacity, especially collaborative capacity, is at a certain level of quality, further investments in the peer culture yield higher-quality implementation, and innovation. After a certain level of capacity has developed, peer cultures really do have the capacity to unleash new ideas. The change leader, then, must recognize this potential and invest in strategies and cultures of internal and external networking. The natural product of this work is two powerful social forces—greater mutual allegiance, and more robust collaborative competition.

In sum, the wisdom of the crowd has huge potential—work the crowd with interactive strategies and you can reap and retain the benefits. The leader's role is still consequential, though it is indirect. Progress and sustainability still require proactive leadership but it involves stimulation, monitoring, feedback, and spreading good ideas and practices. In this way, to motivate the masses, you work both indirectly through peers and directly. Accountability becomes stronger because it is built into group practices, reinforced by transparency. These examples of productive collaboration are small scale compared to what needs to and can happen in the foreseeable future.

In all of the endeavors, myriad change leaders are being generated, largely by leaders developing other leaders. So this is a good time to review the central premise of this book: change leaders are best developed through deliberative practice. Mintzberg (2009), as usual, captures its essence:

1. Managers, let alone leaders, cannot be created in the classroom....

2. Managing is learned on the job enhanced by a variety of experiences....

3. Development programs come in to help managers make meaning of their experiences, by reflecting on it personally and with their colleagues....

4. Intrinsic to this development should be the carrying of the learning back to the workplace, for impact on the organization....

5. All of this has to be organized according to the nature of managing itself. (pp. 227–229)

This work is about quality implementation and pushing innovative frontiers, because it engages the whole group. Despite the compelling evidence cited thus far there is still a general tendency to look to heroic and charismatic leaders or other silver bullets. I suspect that this failure partly comes out of impatience and a sense of urgency, and partly because effective collaborative cultures are not understood. It is likely that fewer than 10% of business organizations have the degree of resolution and collaboration that we are seeking. Confusion reigns, in part because the advice offered by business literature is inconsistent, because it makes common sense complicated, and because the recommendations are so tautological that you can never remember what was key or, practically speaking, even know what it means to follow the advice.

In education, at least, the answer seems clearer—if still elusive in practice. The recent action-based success cases stimulated by Rick DuFour and his colleagues (DuFour, DuFour, Eaker, & Karhanek, 2009) seem pretty straightforward. They put forward three big ideas:

1. A commitment to high levels of learning for all students

2. A commitment to a collaborative culture

3. A commitment to using results to foster continuous improvement (p. 21)

The authors follow with the stories of six named schools, and three named districts, that are doing such work—complete with what they are doing, and how, and with what impact. In all cases we see steady improvement over multiple years, and the results are substantial. Most of these schools increased their learning, as measured by student achievement, by 50% or more.

Despite this, when it comes to addressing the ills of the U.S. public school system—a system that was number one in the world in 1980 and is now about 24th—the initial reform proposals of the Obama administration and Education Secretary Arne Duncan focus on standards, assessments, and individual capacity—almost completely ignoring *collective capacity* (see Fullan, 2010a, for a critique and an alternative). In a recent article I have characterized the problem of education reform as the tendency on the part of leaders to gravitate to four "wrong drivers" (Fullan, 2011b). The wrong drivers (with the corresponding right drivers in parentheses) are accountability (versus capacity building); individual (versus group work); technology (versus pedagogy); and piecemeal (versus systemic). The change leader instinctively selects the combination of right drivers every time, because they are informed by what works in practice to motivate the masses to work together to innovate and to get continuous improvement. The "right drivers" focus directly on changing the culture of the organization and that is why they work.

Collective or collaborative capacity may seem too soft, and certainly it can be, as Hansen (2009) has noted. For the change leader the answer is to realize that *collaborative capacity* is essential, and therefore success is a matter of cultivating the right form of working together. Such work requires focus, discipline, getting the best ideas in place—and yes, it involves competition. Collaboration is not an end in itself but rather involves purposeful, focused working together that gets results precisely because it motivates the masses to innovate and to commit to improvement. Both quality implementation *and* innovation are the strengths of lively peer cultures—they are virtually guaranteed when given a chance.

From the perspective of the change leader, collaboration means that the circle of leadership should always be expanding to incorporate the meaning and motivation of the full group. With resolute leadership and a ready-fire-aim grasp of change in tow, building in collaboration becomes natural. Our change leader knows that social engagement is essential and thus fosters it day after day. By being fully and practically engaged within the organization, leaders always trust the process and their ability to influence it. One of the main reasons that effective leaders trust in their own abilities and those of the group is that they are learners. They have confidence that they can draw on the store of group knowledge to solve many problems, and they are equally confident that they can learn to solve the next one *because they have done it so many times before.* In a word, they learn to learn.

CHAPTER · FIVE

Learn Confidently

*Change Requires Confidence (but True
Confidence Requires Humility)*

Effective change leaders are the most confident people in the room for two reasons. One is that they have a Susan B. Anthony attitude that "failure is impossible." The second is that they and their associates are "learners." They are pretty sure that they can sort out difficult problems even when they don't know in advance exactly how they are going to do it. The key insight for this chapter is

| Key Insight 5 |

Change leaders are more confident than the situation warrants but more humble than they look.

Pfeffer and Sutton (2006, p. 174) captured the gist of this idea with their wonderful definition of wisdom: "Wisdom is the ability to act with knowledge while doubting what you know" (p. 174). Everyone knows that the future is inherently unpredictable. Change leaders are not afraid to enter the unknown if this is required to solve a complex problem, and in so doing they become increasingly comfortable, even excited, about heading into the next change situation. They thus exude more confidence than the situation seems to warrant. Every piece of knowledge and skill they have gained has come from reflective experience. These leaders really do know a hell of a lot. They don't find complexity complex. It's no wonder they are able to motivate the masses.

As a learner, you (the change leader) must do four things in combination:

- Use your brain.

- Cultivate a growth mindset in yourself and in others.

- Be indispensable in the right way.

- Maintain a high level of confidence.

Use Your Brain

The central premise of this book is that when you are in doubt, it's better to examine your practice and that of others who seem to be getting somewhere than it is to reach for the bookshelf. New work on understanding the brain bears out this idea. We know that the brain is best fed through experience. When people *experience* something new, it connects with their feelings first, then their minds. When this leads to new behavior, the latter sticks because it has emotional meaning. This is why I have stressed going from practice to theory.

The astounding things is that the brain can "change itself" through the right kind of experience (Doidge, 2007). Doidge demonstrates that actions can change the actual structure of the brain through a process called *neuroplasticity*. "Trained or stimulated neurons develop 25% more branches and increase their size, the number of connections per neuron, and their blood supply" (p. 43). Life in enriched environments—or, stated differently, drawing on the richness of your environment—develops the brain in adults as well as in babies and children.

In other words, a good experience makes a more lasting impression than a good book. One way to appreciate this fact is to know that actual change is more likely to occur when we are closely involved in doing something. We are more likely to learn from events that we actually experience, as opposed to passively observing something, or hearing about events secondhand.

Dan Goleman (2006), as we saw in the first chapter, takes this a step further in claiming that we are wired to connect socially—that our brain has a propensity to sympathetically mimic actions that we see due to what are called *mirror neurons*. This means that what we see, especially if it has emotional meaning, is literally contagious. Think of the brain, says Doidge, "like a creature with an appetite, one that can grow and change itself through proper nourishment and exercise" (2007, p. 47). One special appetite the brain has is social. This is why the collaborative focus addressed in Chapter Four is vital.

Given all of this, the practical implication for the change leader is to use the core components in Figure 1.1 to stimulate and exercise your own brain and the brains of those you work with. Be deliberative about your practice, work on being a resolute leader, galvanize motivation, build collaboration, and know your impact—and realize that new experiences can have lasting effects. This is what Mintzberg (2004) was getting at when he said that managing "has to be learned ... not just by doing it but by being able to gain conceptual insight *while* doing it" (p. 200, italics original). Although I have been arguing that the experience is the best *source* of new ideas, it doesn't end there. You take the insights into new actions, testing their validity relative to moving the organization forward.

Foster a Growth Mindset

When people point to some leaders as arrogant and others as humble I think they are misdiagnosing the situation. Humility is not all that attractive if it means meekness, timidity, submissiveness, and the like. The key distinction, I think, is whether the leader is a *learner*. Scratch an effective "humble" leader and you will find a confident learner.

I referred in earlier chapters to Carol Dweck's liberating research in which she identifies two fundamentally different mindsets: fixed and growth. People with fixed mindsets think that intelligence and ability are set in stone and can't be changed. They must repeatedly affirm that they are superior. Any setback is labeled as a failure. They avoid risks because failure is seen as a weakness, and they "get their thrill from what's easy—what they have already mastered" (2006, p. 24). Every situation is evaluated in terms of "Will I succeed or fail? Will I look smart or dumb? Will I be accepted or rejected? Will I feel like a winner or loser?" (2006, p. 6). It is easy to see why they don't learn much that is new, because learning involves the risk—and even certainty—of some failure.

The growth mindset is the opposite. People with this orientation believe that they can get better through effort. By trying hard and figuring things out they think they could get smarter: "Not only were they not discouraged by failure, they didn't even think they were failing. They thought they were learning" (Dweck, 2006, p. 6). Risk and effort are worth the possibility of failing because you might learn something, whereas with fixed-mindset people the risk is high because failure would reveal their inadequacies. For growth-oriented people, it is not about immediate perfection, but rather "it is about learning something over time: confronting a challenge and making progress" (p. 24).

Because fixed-mindset people—especially those in positions of power—never want to be wrong, they consistently exude confidence. Confidence, per se, then, is a tricky thing. The scary thought is that the more confident or certain a leader appears, the less right he or she might be. Confidence and being right are not correlated, and thinking you are right is not a strategy.

The good news is that a growth mindset can be cultivated. Dweck and her colleagues have conducted mindset workshops with children in schools and with adults. They focus on "changing the inner monologue from a judgment one to a growth-oriented one" (p. 216). Kids, for example, are told at the beginning of the workshop:

> Many people think that the brain is a mystery. [They] believe
> that a person is born either smart, average or dumb—and
> stays that way for life. But new research shows that the brain
> is more like a muscle—it changes and gets stronger when

you use it.... When you learn new things tiny connections in the brain actually multiply and get stronger. The more you challenge your mind to learn, the more your brain cells grow. ... The result is a stronger smarter brain. (2006, p. 219)

The kids are then given experiences in learning in an atmosphere of nonjudgmentalism. And it works. Kids do alter their mindsets, reinforced by teachers who have been taught how to respond.

More good news, as we saw from Doidge, is that adults can also change their mindsets, and hence their brains. Thus, change leaders must cultivate in themselves this capacity to admit and learn from mistakes. By knowing the mindsets and your personality you can catch yourself "in the throes of a fixed mindset"—such as getting discouraged when something requires a lot of effort—and resolve to learn more and keep going (Dweck, 2006, p. 46).

Change leaders also need to help develop growth-oriented mindsets in those they are mentoring. But just as it is hard for individual leaders to admit mistakes, it is equally difficult—especially for resolute leaders in a hurry—to be nonjudgmental as they relate to organization problems. Thus, leaders have to name the "risk-taking" norm (for example, "We value an open, learn-from-mistakes culture"), and model it time and time again in practice.

We are now talking about trust. People believe something when they have witnessed and experienced it repeatedly—just as they can smell rhetoric and lip service a mile away. Trust is an outcome of modeling—proving yourself through your action over time. Being open is a powerful step in the right direction.

Tim Brighouse, whom I consider to be the educational change czar in England for the past four decades, takes this even further. His advice for young leaders: "Learn to say I don't know when you actually don't know the answer, and learn to take the blame even if it isn't your fault so that you don't hang people out to dry" (Fullan, 2010b, p. 14). In this way, the leader demonstrates that he or she is both learner and protector.

Speaking of growth, we often forget what it is like at the very *beginning* of one's leadership career. This struck me recently when we were preparing some case study training materials for the National College for Leadership of Schools and Children's Services in England. The training was to help new school heads in their development, and we were working with two accomplished school heads, testing the leadership qualities of effective leaders against their experiences. There was a good match between the leadership qualities that we identified as critical (such as those in Figure 1.1) and how these two accomplished principals went about their work. But someone thought to ask, "What was it like when *you* were in your first headship?" Well that was a different story. One said:

> I was keen to make sure I was well prepared. I spent the entire summer in a state of anxious excitement. I focused for hours on drafting and re-drafting how I was going to handle the first staff meeting.... [But] when the real work began it became clear that the task was enormous. The actual ethos of the school was a million miles from my values and aspirations. It was a toxic environment in which a powerful group of staff drawn from all levels of leadership, including the senior team, ran the school outside the formal structures,

often in spite of what had been agreed by staff and senior leaders.

The other school head told us about her first job as principal when a group of parents circulated a petition objecting to her selection (because a popular internal candidate was passed over).

These two school heads are now accomplished and recognized in the country as highly effective school leaders—but they didn't start that way. I would venture to say that they evolved successfully because they had Dweck's growth mindset; they were learners. It is essential then that both new leaders and those who mentor them recognize and embrace the cultivation of the habits of the learning mind, appreciating that when people start that they have a lot to learn. Only the learners eventually become effective change leaders.

Still more good news: it is actually more effective to be transparent about mistakes and what you have to learn. People know that humans are not perfect, and they will typically readily forgive leaders who screw up and admit it—whereas they hate a cover-up, the biggest trust-buster there is. Even in selfish terms you end up looking and doing better when you admit your mistakes. And these days, with access to information almost a given, you are almost always better off being open about what you are doing and the problems (and successes) you are encountering.

Be Indispensable in the Right Way

Indispensable leaders are dangerous for the obvious reason that when they inevitably leave, the organization will suffer a setback. At the organizational level, a company that works at leadership development in the right way can create a culture that makes indispensability obsolete. Crutchfield and McLeod Grant (2007), for example, report that sharing leadership and empowering others was one of six practices evident in high-impact nonprofit organizations. In particular, they found that

> [strong leadership] extends throughout the [successful] organization. CEOs of high-impact non-profits share a commitment that goes beyond their own egos, and use their leadership to empower others. (p. 156)

Personally, I don't think it has anything to do with going beyond one's ego, but rather recognizing that the ego is not the only thing that needs to be satisfied. The resolute leader builds the guiding coalition and helps develop leadership throughout the organization because that is the best way to have impact. What could be more ego gratifying than that! Thus, creating ever-widening circles of leadership is the main role of the change leader. You can have your cake and eat it too on this one—be proud of your accomplishments and extend your impact into the future.

When McKinsey & Co. (Mourshed, Chinezi, & Barber, 2010) studied school systems (countries, states, provinces) that had success in going from good to great and were sustaining their effectiveness, they found three factors that were critical to greater longevity of high performance. One was the establishment of collaborative practices (as seen in our Chapter Four, collaboration today fuels the future). The second was the development of a supportive infrastructure that can provide continuous development and monitoring. The third factor (our point here) was "architecting tomorrow's leadership": "the successful systems actively foster the development of the next generation of system leadership from within ensuring that there is a continuity of purpose and vision" (p. 28).

Crutchfield and McLeod Grant also found that leaders who share leadership had "extraordinarily long tenure" (2007, p. 167). Great leaders last longer—which, again, is satisfying to the self. I could say that for most of us it is always better to do a job that you are personally satisfied with (and even to think that no one else could have been quite so successful) while at the same time helping to develop others. It is OK to feel important as long as you are proactively developing other leaders. The best kind of indispensability is when your leadership actions develop others, when you do good things together for long periods of time, and when others are in a better position to carry on after you leave—*in short, be indispensable to the future, so to speak, because of what you do today.*

Be Confident

Change leadership, as Mintzberg (2009) observes, is not for the "feint-hearted" (sic) or insecure (p. 185). That may have been a typo, but I prefer to see it as a play on words—change leaders indeed must not "feint." Rather, decisiveness is key. Any leader, continues Mintzberg, who is "inclined to avoid problems, pass them on, or simply cover their own rear ends, can make things dreadful for everyone else" (p. 185). But he also finds that the supremely confident can be even worse. Bear in mind, he says, "the shaky foundation on which such confidence can lie: information about which the manager is never sure, issues loaded with ambiguities, conundrums that can never be resolved, forcing the manager to [sometimes] 'wing it'" (p. 185).

But the fact is that people want and need confidence from their leaders, especially when times are dangerous and in a very real sense unpredictable. Thus, the change leader, to be effective, has to act with more confidence than the situation warrants. You have this confidence because the issues are so vital (you have to hope, no matter what; failure is impossible), and because you know that you and the group are damn good learners and problem solvers, chances are you will succeed.

This is a delicate balance, to be sure. Slip into too many "I don't knows" and the group begins to lose confidence in you (and you lose confidence in you). Get too confident, perhaps because of success and constant kudos, and you might stop listening and learning. Mintzberg calls it the "Clutch of Confidence" conundrum: "how to maintain a level of confidence without crossing over into arrogance" (2009, p. 186). This requires reflective practice and feedback from trusted others.

Part of the solution is attitudinal:

> The big lesson is that the best leaders are smart enough to act like they are in charge but wise enough not to let their power go to their heads or to take themselves too seriously. (Pfeffer & Sutton, 2006, p. 214)

We often think that being in complete charge of ourselves and the situation is a good thing. Dan Thurmon (2010) says this is not reality. Recognize that things are never perfect and learn from being "off balance on purpose" (the subtitle of his book is *Embrace Uncertainty and Create a Life You Love*). Thurmon says we live one moment at a time in a world that is unpredictable, so that by definition we will never be in a state of balance for long. Balance, he maintains, is both unattainable and undesirable, so work on your purpose in life, but treat its pursuit as a matter of learning and leaning forward. Balance is undesirable, according to Thurmon, because it represents stagnation, sameness, and protecting what is imaginary or unrealistic, and ultimately amounts to having a little of everything. By contrast, "off balance" represents growth and action, change, embracing what might be real, and having more of what really matters (Thurmon, 2010, p. 15). If dynamism is reality you might as well approach it as an off-balance proposition from which you constantly learn.

From the change perspective, uncertainty works because, as we have seen throughout this book, the change leader has a number of anchors: purpose, deliberate learning, patterns deriving from collaborative learning, and so on. What gives leaders resolve is that in the best organizations there is a strong element of moral purpose in the equation. The values embedded in respecting and wanting change—integrity, respect, and faith in others, commitment to bringing humankind to a higher level of accomplishment, and even appreciating that individuals and groups are not perfect—all have a moral base. Resolute leadership is morally driven, but it is also change-savvy driven.

If the change is so important morally, then figuring out how to enact it is equally crucial. In effect, what change leaders do is to *change context*. A frequent adage in the change literature is that "context is everything." If that is so, change leadership is about how to move individuals, organizations, and systems into new contexts. It is about changing context for the better. Change the situation, and you often get different behavior (Heath & Heath, 2010). Change leaders need to be explicitly aware that this is the business they are in.

The change leaders we have seen in this book are especially effective because they change other leaders around them, who in turn change each other. You can see this in York Region where literally thousands of change leaders have redefined the context—the very system within which they work (Sharratt & Fullan, 2009). And the same is true of the Mayo Clinic, Four Seasons Hotels, McKinsey & Co.'s school systems "that keep getting better," and all other organizations that are on the move, never achieving or wanting to achieve a steady balance.

When you let your practice and the practices of others who appear to be doing better than you drive your thinking and associated actions, you are entering new territory. But because these actions are grounded in actual practice, steps taken are not nearly as risky as the leap of faith required in trying to make the abstract advice of management books a reality.

Let practice—informed by research and theory—be your guide. But be your own interpreter. Approach each day with a growth mindset. Do this for a few years, and you will become incredibly change savvy. Helping others develop will add to your knowledge and impact. Be so confident that you can afford to be humble, and you will learn even more. In short, use your brain!

But would that it be a simple matter to use your brain. As we will see in the next chapter, it turns out that it is damn hard to know yourself. You are going to have to learn some techniques that enable you to dig more deeply within yourself. This will help you both know and improve your impact.

CHAPTER · SIX

Know Your Impact

Drowning in Data, Thirsty for Knowledge

Deliberative practice puts you in the right arena for learning. Resolute leadership keeps you in the game. Impressive empathy and other motivational actions that "walk the walk" motivate the masses. Purposeful collaboration provides focus for the actual work, and garners innovation as it generates mutual allegiance and productive competition. Learning confidently requires knowing what is going on and what impact you are having. In doing all of this a lot of data come your way, and that turns out to a mixed blessing. For this chapter's key insight I borrow from the Hopper brothers (2009, p. 125).

Key Insight 6
Statistics are a wonderful servant and an appalling master.

But it's worse than that. Heaps of research in social psychology prove beyond a shadow of a doubt that our brain distorts things in ways that we are not aware of. To be effective you are going to have to go out of your way to get to know yourself.

Consider the titles of recent books summarizing much of this research: *On Being Certain: Believing You Are Right Even When You're Not* (Burton, 2008); *The Invisible Gorilla: And Other Ways Our Intuitions Deceive Us* (Chabris & Simons, 2010). *Why We Make Mistakes: How We Look Without Seeing, Forget Things in Seconds, and Are All Pretty Sure We Are Way Above Average* (Hallinan, 2009); *Distracted: The Erosion of Attention and the Coming Dark Age* (Jackson, 2009), and *Mistakes Were Made (But Not by Me): Why We Justify Foolish Beliefs, Bad Decisions, and Hurtful Acts* (Tavris & Aronson, 2007). The titles alone humble one.

One theme in this research is that we don't see even obvious things unless we are looking for them (or more precisely unless we are used to looking for them). That's why we run over bicycles and cut off motorcycles more than cars. We literally don't expect them and thus don't see them even when we should. The most famous experiment concerns the invisible gorilla (Chabris & Simons, 2010). These authors made a short film of two teams—one dressed in black, the other in white—passing around a basketball. Viewers were asked to count the number of passes that were made in the film clip. The correct answer was 34, and most people did well on the test. Then the authors asked the viewers whether they had seen anything unusual in the film. About half said no. They then replayed the film. In fact in the middle of the clip a female student dressed in a gorilla suit walked into the scene, stopped in the middle of the players, faced the camera, and thumped her chest, and then walked off, spending nine seconds on screen. Yet half the viewers did not notice it! Indeed this is not a bad thing for our purposes. Most people tuned out the gorilla because it was irrelevant to the task. One could speculate that those who did not notice the gorilla are better at task completion. Focus is thus a good thing given the countless distractions that come our way. Of course, being oblivious to danger is another matter.

Irrelevant distractions, and we haven't even introduced the digital world yet. The volume and ubiquity of technology presents great new possibilities and dangers—the latter all the more insidious because they are invisible. Jackson (2009) puts it this way: "The way we live is eroding our capacity for deep, sustained, perceptive attention—the building block of intimacy, wisdom, and cultural progress" (p. 13). When longtime technophiles like Nicholas Carr (2010) start to have doubts, we all should worry. Concerned that his "use of the Internet might be changing the way my brain was processing information" (p. 38), Carr examined the research and came to this conclusion:

> The news is even more disturbing than I suspected. Dozens of studies by psychologists, neurobiologists, educators, and Web designers point to the same conclusion: when we go online, we enter an environment that promotes cursory reading, hurried and distracted thinking, and superficial learning. (pp. 115–116)

As neurobiologists have found, barraging our short-term memory with information overloads it to the point where the capacity for transferring to long-term memory is seriously compromised. The more attention-demanding tasks the brain engages in, the worse it does. In other words, multitaskers are good at quantity, not quality. The key to long-term memory is attentiveness, which is the very quality that goes missing when people are drowning in data (Carr, p. 103).

This body of research also shows that not only do we suffer from cognitive impairment, but our capacity to relate to others also suffers: "It's not only deep thinking that requires a calm, attentive mind. It's also empathy and compassion.... The higher emotions emerge from neural processes that are inherently slow" (Carr, p. 220).

It is important to note that these warnings (backed up by considerable hard evidence) are coming from many of the pioneers of the new technology. It is not turning out the way they envisaged. As Lanier (2010) says, "When my friends and I built the first virtual reality machines, the whole point was to make this world more creative, expressive, empathic, and interesting. It was not to escape it" (p. 33). Lanier continues, "We were supposed to invent better fundamental types of expression: not just movies, but interactive virtual worlds; not just games, but simulations with moral and aesthetic profundity. That's why I was criticizing the old way of doing things" (p. 131). Rushkoff (2010) says, "program or be programmed," as he fears the subtle dominance of the Internet over us.

So what does all of this mean for us as change leaders?

The technophiles who worry about the unintended con-sequences of the digital world—Carr, Lanier, Rushkoff, and others—do not advocate that we abandon technology (which is impossible anyway), but rather that we become more con-scious and wary in the face of its onslaught, and more proactive in controlling our use of the World Wide Web. This advice is deeply compatible with the theme of the change leaders that

I have been building. Use your brain; let deliberate practice drive better practice. Motivate the masses so that they can innovate and provide checks and balances for what to retain. Be aware and cognizant of your impact. Know what you are looking for by way of evidence, and maintain your capacity to be surprised. Work hard at getting to know yourself. In other words, be a learner.

To help with learning, effective change leaders integrate and use data about practice and outcomes, which allows them to cause and to mark progress. Technology has made this resource simultaneously more powerful and more dangerous. How do we prevent the cure from becoming the disease?

The Disease

We have just discussed the nature of the "disease of distraction." Change leaders need to focus on a small number of quantitative and qualitative measures of impact and use these as a core part of the strategy of moving even further. And with all the data flying around these days they have to be good at deciding what *not* to do. It is easy to get overloaded, confused, and misdirected by too much information.

The research referred to above reports experiment after experiment that finds a string of common points:

- Most of us (men more so) tend to be overconfident.

- Memory is more often reconstruction rather than reproduction.

- Our conscious short term memory is confined to 5–7 things at once.

- Multitasking is subject to error.

- We skim a lot and miss what in retrospect seems obvious.

- We sincerely believe things from the past that are simply not true; we provide explanations of the past or the present that put ourselves in a good light, and others less so.

- After a point, more information makes people less accurate than having less information (the overload problem).

- We don't like to make mistakes but we dislike even more admitting them.

- Our best lies are ones that we firmly believe to be true.

- Confidence may be negatively related to accuracy and in any case is no predictor that you have something right.

- And worst of all, a lot of this occurs in our subconscious brain, so that "introspection alone will not help our vision, because it will simply confirm our self-justifying beliefs" (Tavris & Aronson, 2007, p. 44).

As Burton (2008, p. xiii) puts it, "Despite how certainty feels . . . it [often arises] out of involuntary brain mechanisms that, like love or anger, function independently of reason." Feelings are far more memorable than rational thoughts, and—this is crucial—we are especially vulnerable to distortion. Remember the Elephant and the Rider. Well, it turns out that the Elephant has a great memory, but not necessarily a good one.

If we apply this to the change leader, the path to successful change is a minefield that will require careful checks and balances. Let us move closer to the use of data. Pfeffer and Sutton (2000) name "when measurement obstructs good judgment" (p. 139) as one of the major barriers to closing the knowing-doing gap. They document three big problems. The first occurs when organizations focus on "short-term, high stakes financial targets" (people become shortsighted, self-centered, and often cheat). The second is "overly complex measures" that overload and confuse the organization. (They name one bank that has six main measures with over 20 submeasures—and because there are too many measures, none of them are taken seriously.) The third happens when in-process measures are neglected in favor of outcome measures (how well you have done). But without in-process measures you cannot "understand what is going right and what is going wrong" (p. 154).

Mintzberg (2009) furnishes a similar warning when he talks about "the soft underbelly of hard data." Hard data, he says, is often limited in scope, excessively aggregated, arrives too late, and is sometimes just plain unreliable (pp. 177–178). The message for change leaders is simple: take hard data into account, but don't be mesmerized by the numbers. The cure is deeper than that—but to be effective it can't be too complex.

The Cure

The cure, for starters, is mainly in your head; it's what you do to protect yourself from inevitable distortions. The brain on its own is naive. It literally suffers from knowing a lot but not being able to identify what is best in a given situation. It doesn't know what it doesn't know—but thinks it does. Therefore, the solutions are habits of the mind and corresponding mechanisms to detect and correct falsehoods. The main features are shown in Exhibit 6.1.

Exhibit 6.1: Cures for the Distorted Brain

1. Practice being humble; admit your mistakes.
2. Tighten the action-feedback loop.
3. Establish a climate of openness and critical feedback.
4. Focus on a few core priorities and doing them well.
5. Develop and hone your skills for getting to know yourself.
6. Introduce and honor the humble checklist.
7. Celebrate success after it happens, not before.

Let's look at these "cures" one by one.

Admit Your Mistakes

We all give lip service to the importance of admitting our mistakes, but few of us practice it. I have already cited Carol Dweck's important work (2006) on the two "mindsets"—one that sees that sees mistakes as personal flaws, and the other as learning experiences. Those with the former mindset get stuck; the latter get better and better. These are our change leaders. But the consequences go beyond the individual leader. The whole organization suffers or gains by how the leader responds when things go wrong.

Pfeffer and Sutton (2006) say that "if you look at how the most effective systems in the world are managed, a hallmark is that when something goes wrong, people face the hard facts, learn what happened and why, and keep using those facts to make the system better" (p. 232). Getting at facts in an open and timely fashion is knowing your impact as you go, and doing something to make it better.

Tighten the Action-Feedback Loop

Second, align goals, action, and feedback. When data are closely aligned to the goals of resolute leadership, subject to the discipline of the change process, and processed through collaboration, they are not just end measures—they are part and parcel of knowing and getting success. Good data must be treated fundamentally as central to *strategy* and not just seen as an accountability measure. One of the best ways to cure overconfidence is to establish systems of "quick, corrective feedback" (Hallinan, 2009, p. 158). With all the emphasis on accountability these days it is reassuring to realize that the best way of improving performance inside the organization also serves the accountability requirement quite well. Put another way, if you have a transparent evidenced-based process under way you can more readily manage the external demands from boards of directors or government agencies.

Michael Barber (2007) applied this logic to his complex and mammoth task in Tony Blair's Prime Minister's Delivery Unit (PMDU). As head of PMDU Michael was responsible for improvements in health, education, crime, and transportation for all England. His approach was (1) to avoid micromanagement; unnecessary bureaucracy; short-termism; opinion without evidence; and (2) to emphasize in turn plain speaking; early identification of problems, data, and evidence; application of best practice; building capacity; and so on (p. 65). One data rule Barber followed was never ask for information from a department that it should not already want and use itself. Barber kept the data close to both process and outcomes essentially to spur success.

Ontario built its system reform strategy on action-feedback in 2003 when it started down the path of system transformation of the public school system. The government arm's-length agency, the Education Quality and Accountability Office (EQAO) had an information system based on testing students. The problem was that the EQAO system was detached from action, and as such was suspect among teachers and principals. Two things were changed—and the sequence is crucial.

First the government stated that it would begin to form partnerships with districts and schools based on respect for the teaching profession and identification of effective instructional practices (in this case, in literacy and numeracy). Action and related data would drive implementation. Three years were spent developing this on the ground, which meant that (1) more trust was established, and (2) good practices were identified and developed, and thus there were more valuable things to share.

Second, three years later the government established a usable and transparent assessment system called Statistical Neighbors, which organized and made the information available on all six scores (reading, writing, and mathematics in grades 3 and 6)—first to the education sector and second to the public at large. The strategy called for a careful organization of the data so that schools were grouped according to similar demographic and socioeconomic (hence, statistical neighbors).

As part of the same evolution the strategy entailed developing capacities in schools and districts to (1) diagnose student learning needs on an individualized ongoing basis, (2) link these needs to specific instructional improvements designed to address the learning needs, and (3) track improvements according to annual EQAO results. Successful schools and districts, that is, those showing the most cumulative achievement in literacy and numeracy, also showed the greatest capacity gains in their ability to use data.

Integrated models like this work very well. The idea is to link practice and outcomes by focusing on a small number of key items within which the linkage can be already seen, understood, and assessed. Once again, we are back to common sense—to practice driving outcomes.

The development and sharing of pinpointed information systems linked to new action is integral to the success of all effective organizations. Gittell (2009), in her study of high-performing health care institutions, devotes a whole chapter to "developing shared information systems." Only two of the nine hospitals that Gittell studied had "fully automated information systems regarding a patient's current condition, inpatient procedures or outpatient consults" (p. 174). She found that doubling the inclusiveness of information systems produced a 15% increase in relational coordination among nurses, physicians, residents, therapists, case managers, and social workers (p. 181). Further, Gittell writes:

> Specifically, inclusive information systems produce shorter hospital stays and higher levels of patient satisfaction, along with some of the most substantial improvements in clinical outcomes of any of the work practices we have experienced. (p. 183)

It is important to emphasize that it is not the increasing presence of greater information technology (IT) capacity or the increased demands for external accountability that lead to greater success, but rather when IT is used to help the organization focus on its own operations and how they can be improved. As organizations get on the move, members seek better and better knowledge with IT at their service.

Establish a Climate of Openness and Critical Feedback

Third, if you want transparency, climate is crucial. Norms that encourage and value critical feedback from all team members, especially from those with less status, are essential. More than one airliner has crashed, and more than one patient has died, in circumstances where a junior member of the team knew that something was wrong—even very wrong—but failed to speak up or was ignored. Thirty years ago flying was more dangerous because cockpit norms were such that junior members of the team did not feel free to speak up even if they thought something was wrong. Hallinan (2009, p. 195) cites the 1978 crash of a United Airlines DC-8 near Portland, Oregon, in which the plane simply ran out of fuel six miles short of the airport. The flight engineer knew the fuel was running out but because of cockpit norms did not speak up and tell the captain. Several other documented dangerous and fatal cases from the 1970s and 1980s have resulted in entirely new norms in the cockpit.

Teamwork has changed more in cockpits than in surgical theaters. In a survey of three countries, pilots and doctors were asked whether junior staff members should be free to question decisions made by senior staff members. Ninety-seven percent of the pilots responded yes, compared to 55% of surgeons

(Hallinan, pp. 194–195). If failure to speak up when something is amiss is difficult in life-or-death situations imagine how much good feedback gets lost in regular day-to-day situations.

Focus on a Few Priorities and Doing Them Well

People can't remember, let alone cope, with multiple change initiatives. If you add the deluge of information that automatically comes with all the newly accessible technology, the flood becomes overwhelming. Doug Reeves (2010) warns of "the law of innovation fatigue." Abrahamson (2004) calls it "repetitive change syndrome" and says that it brings with it "initiative overload," "change-related chaos," and "widespread employee anxiety, cynicism, and burnout" (pp. 2–3). David Rock (2009) shows how easily and naturally the brain gets overloaded and impairs our performance.

In contrast, we saw in earlier chapters that successful change leaders focus on a few core priorities and are resolute about them, and this can have a powerful combined impact on both performance and morale.

Develop and Hone Techniques for Getting to Know Yourself

Getting feedback from others will help but it is not nearly enough because evidently it is hard to get to know oneself. Enter the Elephant again (for a big guy he gets around). Daft (2010) devotes a whole book to recognizing and reconciling your "divided self," which consists of *the executive* (our consciousness), and *the inner elephant* (the strength of unconscious systems and habits).

We saw earlier in this chapter how humans are prone to distort reality. Daft reports additional evidence that humans have a tendency to "react too quickly, think too inflexibly, want too much control, feel emotional avoidance or attraction, exaggerate the future, and seek satisfaction in the wrong places" (2010, p. 53).

Daft recommends over a dozen techniques that he talks about under the label of "try this." They all involve relaxing and getting in touch with yourself. Some are task oriented, such as steps for "visualizing your intention" (for example, sit comfortably, visualize yourself completing a familiar task, select a task toward which you feel some resistance), and a procedure to "review the day" with 10 steps (for example, find a quiet place, recall events that went well, dwell on situations you would like to improve).

Others involve meditation such as "mindful meditation" (for example, sit quietly, focus on your breath in the present moment, expand awareness to thoughts and feelings), and "practice forgiveness meditation" (for example, bring to mind a person and situation in which you felt upset, visualize it and feel your negative thoughts, visualize yourself not being annoyed).

Many of us will feel uncomfortable with such Eastern philosophy "mind games" but the evidence on how the subconscious brain distorts reality is so overwhelming that the best advice is to try a few of these techniques and see what you think. Consistent with the theme of my book, Daft's goal is to see how we can work more effectively "from the inside out" (2010, p. 287).

Introduce and Honor the Humble Checklist

We find further help in an unexpected place: the lowly checklist. For instance, the checklist, along with training in team-based communication in the cockpit, has transformed safety in the airline industry. In the past 10 years fatal crashes of airplanes have declined 65% in the United States (Hallinan, 2009, p. 193).

Progress is also being made in the medical field, despite stubborn pushback. The surgeon-writer Atul Gawande (2010) gives us a fascinating, troubling, and ultimately encouraging account of the role of checklists in the medical field. At a high level, the advice amounts to getting into a "use your brain" habit, aided by the checklist. For example, in 2001, Peter Pronovost, a critical care specialist at Johns Hopkins Hospital, created a simple checklist for preventing central line infections. (A *central line* is a catheter that is passed through a vein into the vena cava, or the right atrium, of the heart.) The checklist included five steps: (1) wash your hands with soap, (2) clean the patient's skin with chlorhexidine antiseptic, (3) put sterile drapes over the entire patient, (4) wear a mask, hat, sterile gown, and gloves, and (5) put a sterile dressing over the insertion site once the line is in. It's hard to believe, but before the advent of the checklist, data showed that at least one of these steps was omitted in about one-third of cases. When the checklist procedure was installed—and monitored—within one year at the study sites the infection rate dropped from 11% to zero. Basically, this checklist aids recall in much the same way as a cockpit checklist helps pilots make sure everything is good to go before takeoff. The checklist also empowers observers who notice a misstep to call a stop in the line insertion process.

Pronovost later initiated a larger project in nine Michigan hospitals. With careful monitoring and troubleshooting (people forget to use checklists, even those with only five steps), during the first 18 months these hospitals saved 1,500 lives (and $175 million) as infections dramatically dropped, "all because of a stupid little checklist," says Gawande (p. 44). Gawande does not specify how the money was saved but presumably through a combination of not having to redo procedures and reduced lawsuits. Checklists reduce mistakes by ensuring that key elements are covered.

Gawande and his team decided to try the checklist idea on a larger scale. They developed a three-part set of checklists for surgeries. Part one addressed steps to be taken before anesthesia (seven checks). Part two applied to actions after anesthesia but before incision (seven more checks). And part three came at the end of the operation (five checks).

Eight hospitals were recruited for the trial, four in high-income countries (Canada, the United States, England, and New Zealand), the other four in poorer countries (Jordan, India, the Philippines, and Tanzania). All Gawande's team did, so to speak, was to introduce a three-step, 19-item checklist and show people how to use it, including how to monitor the implementation of the steps—while stressing that it was just a simple tool to improve results. The results were amazing. Surgical complications fell by 36% across the eight hospitals, infections were cut in half, and deaths fell by 47%.

Can checklists help change leaders in other businesses? First, let's review Gawande's criteria for good checklists. He says that basically checklists must be "simple, measurable and transmissible" (p. 70). Bad checklists, he notes, are vague, imprecise, too long, hard to use, and impractical. Good checklists are "precise, efficient, to the point, and easy to use in even the most difficult situations" (p. 120). They have to be tested in the real world. They are, he says, "quick and simple tools aimed to buttress the skills of expert professionals" (p. 128).

Gawande also has an answer for more complex tasks that he found in the building industry. If the detailed steps cannot be specified in advance, then what is required is communication checkpoints to make sure that people speak to one another "on X date about Y process" (p. 65). The mere act of requiring team members to stop and talk to one another before proceeding could be valuable.

If we then imagine a checklist for change leaders it may look like Exhibit 6.2.

Exhibit 6.2: Sample Checklist for Change Leaders

☐ Do I have a small number of core priorities?

☐ What am I doing to communicate with organization members both initially and especially on an ongoing basis?

☐ Have I stopped to see if I am practicing impressive empathy in relation to potential naysayers?

☐ Have I spelled out the norm of speaking up when there are persistent problems, and provided opportunities for people to identify problems?

☐ Are we gathering data that are simple, ongoing, and used for quick feedback on how well things are going? Are our data helping us focus or are we drowning in it?

☐ Have I specified when the team needs to meet periodically to discuss progress and problem solve? In the past six months, have I stopped to acknowledge mistakes publicly, and to learn from them?

☐ Do I regularly practice reflective techniques to get to know my inner self?

Without such a mindset and system of checks we are likely to experience detached, fragmented, incomplete, overloaded, or inaccessible information systems that seem to be the norm in most organizations.

Celebrate Success After It Happens, Not Before

The final element of Exhibit 6.1 is to celebrate success. Once you and others know your impact, only after success is achieved to some degree can you truly celebrate success. This is what I call the energizing power of "realization" (Fullan, 2011a). Celebration is authentic only *after* you have something to show for it.

This takes us back to the ongoing galvanization of motivation that was the subject of Chapter Three. When success is practice driven you always know whether you have something to show for your efforts. Walking the walk and being close to knowing your impact will give you specific things to cherish.

This phenomenon of needing to know your impact is captured nicely in Patrick Lencioni's *The Three Signs of a Miserable Job* (2007). Everyone knows what a miserable job is, says Lencioni:

> It's the one you dread going to and can't wait to leave. It's the one that saps your energy even when you're not busy. It's the one that makes you go home at the end of the day with less enthusiasm and more cynicism than you had when you left in the morning. (p. 210)

The three signs of misery at work, according to Lencioni, are anonymity, irrelevance, and immeasurement. Resolute leaders engaged in a dynamic change process while building collaborative practice help create personal identity and collective meaning (that is, relevance) with those in the organization. Once the work is meaningful, people become interested in the results of their efforts, and results in turn furnish more meaning.

Knowing your impact is central to management because it is leaders who need to guide improvement in a way that organization members find meaningful. I hope it is clear that leaders will never enjoy impact if employees are not finding it. An amazing side effect, argues Lencioni, is that

> employees themselves begin to take a greater interest in their colleagues, help them finding meaning and relevance in their work, and find better ways to gauge their own success. (p. 225)

We don't have to get mysterious about all of this. What it does is take us back to where I started—day-to-day leaders and managers focusing on a small number of key things, doing them well, and being transparent about their practice and progress. The more you do it, the more you will come to trust the process, and the more you can confirm that trust by knowing the impact that you are having. It is enough to make you confident to do even more. It's simplexity itself, really.

CHAPTER · SEVEN

Sustain Simplexity

Just Right Simple

C omplex is not necessarily the same as complicated. Management is neither as complicated nor as simple as the business literature would have us believe. If you read widely in the business field you will be struck with what seems like a lot of common sense (and if you look closely you will discern a lot of contradictory messages), but with little retentive clarity—striving for complexity but achieving clutter, as I call it. Mintzberg, Ahlstrand, and Lampel (2010) came up with a composite list of 52 "basic qualities for assured managerial effectiveness" (p. 8). Now, that is complicated.

Key Insight 7

Simplexity is salvation for an intricate world.

I have extracted only seven big-picture qualities, which we will revisit shortly. They are not difficult to grasp—that's the simple part of simplexity. What is complex is becoming good at combining them—doing them all at the same time—in the setting where you work. Instead of wasting your time searching for answers elsewhere, start with your own practice. There is only one shift you need to make at the beginning, and that is to begin to treat your own practice as your crucible for learning. Once you commit to the notion that you earn and learn your managerial stripes through your own deliberative action, you are off to the races. And you are the rider.

Using practice as the lever of learning gets you into a progressive learning mode. The evidence is clear—be a deliberate learner in any field and you will become damn good in about ten years. As you go you need to help the next generation of learners become damn good.

As a first step toward improving your own managerial effectiveness, I suggest that you start by linking your own practice to the seven key insights identified across the chapters (Exhibit 7.1). Dwell on each of these insights in turn to consider what you have learned about your own change leadership.

In the course of the book I have provided seven key insights, shown in Exhibit 7.1.

Exhibit 7.1: The Key insights

- The effective change leader actively participates as a learner in helping the organization improve.
- Effective change leaders combine resolute moral purpose with impressive empathy.
- Realized effectiveness is what motivates people to do more.
- Collaborative competition is the yin and yang of successful change.
- Change leaders are more confident than the situation warrants but more humble than they look.
- Statistics are a wonderful servant and an appalling master.
- Simplexity is salvation for an intricate world.

We saw that change leaders "show up." They participate with others in mutual learning (Insight 1). Now, apply this to yourself. Would those who report to you and your peers call you a participating learner in the life of your organization? What more could you do to demonstrate this quality?

We saw also that change leaders never give up, but at the same time they have an impressive empathy with others, even those with whom they might disagree (Insight 2). They use their persistence to be clear about what they stand for, but they are very much aware that "being right" is not a strategy. They know that the complexity part of the change equation entails building relationships with a variety of others who may not agree with them at the beginning. Their respectful approach allows them to teach as well as learn from others. What is your track record of building relationships with people who initially disagreed with you?

Change leaders know that talk is cheap and that front-end visions are overrated. It is when ideals are "realized" in practice that they become truly motivational (Insight 3). More than that, they recognize that realizing success—not just achieving success but understanding how it happens—is the key to sustainability. New energy comes from getting better at something that represents an important value. Under your leadership, how much have you and your people actually accomplished—and did people mark progress as proof that they can and want to do more?

Collaboration is crucial, but you must open it to ideas from others, and to competition with them (Insight 4). Does your collaboration extend beyond your own unit? Have you been conscious that you are both building greater mutual allegiance with wider and wider groups and at the same time enjoying the experience and fruits of friendly competition?

Confidence in the face of overwhelming challenges is essential and compatible with humility (Insight 5). Humility is always a quality of change leaders who have deeper confidence because they trust that they and the group will figure it out. Do you have a good balance between confidence and humility?

The Hopper brothers (2009) provide Insight 6: information abounds and can sometimes be more confusing than ignorance—but data are a necessary and wonderful servant when used well. We also saw that when you know what you are looking for—when you are focused—any task becomes more manageable. Good data serve both strategic and accountability functions. Is your organization inundated with data, or is what you use nicely integrated with your actions and assessment of progress?

Having simplexity as your change mantra allows you to tackle complex problems without feeling overwhelmed (Insight 7). Have you avoided making things too simple, or unnecessarily abstract and complicated—"just right" simplexity is what you want.

The key insights are a good natural way of focusing on improving your change leadership capacities. If you can attend to these seven things in concert you would not miss much. This is the way of simplexity.

The Change Leader Framework

At the same time, it will not do any harm to reinforce the idea that understanding the seven elements of the change leader framework will make you a better leader (Figure 7.1).

Figure 7.1: The Change Leader

I am not suggesting that you apply the framework to your situation but rather that you consider where you are in your own practice and then relate it outward to the frame. Let's review:

- **Be Resolute.** You know that you have to be in for the long haul when you realize that all effective change leaders face huge challenges, especially in the early stages of a new initiative. Patience and persistence when things are not going well are essential, and are at the heart of resolute leadership.

- **Motivate the Masses.** The payoff begins to come as leaders engage others by understanding that commitment to change is generated through purposeful action. Leaders create conditions for others to develop ownership through doing. When ownership is achieved on some scale, it rubs off on others, thereby creating shared commitment.

- **Collaborate to Compete.** Once you get going, the power of collaboration represents one of the best "pressure and support" combinations around. The benefits of collective commitment and push for greater performance begin to take hold. The masses get motivated.

- **Learn Confidently.** Being a confident learner all the while is the basic underpinning that enables success. Here we have Dweck's growth mindset (2006) where learning in the face of challenges is seen as natural, and success is not expected every time. It is complexity that presents the most intrinsically interesting situation for the change leaders. And rendering it to solvable proportions gives the most satisfaction.

- **Know Your Impact.** The two-way street between action and knowing your impact is essential and tricky for it is easy to be misled by data, and to miss vital elements. Getting lean and specific in the use of data is a key skill in the glutted information age.

- **Practice Drives Theory** and **Sustain Simplexity.** These two elements provide a foundation for the other five core elements of the change framework. The argument in this book has been to return change leadership to its natural habitat—what do people do every day and how can we improve it. When you learn in situ, and from other "situs," what you learn is necessarily grounded and practical. Along the way you can test what you are learning against research and theories. This way you have a more natural progression of learning to become a more effective change leader.

We get significant corroboration for the change framework in Adam Bryant's (2011) up-close study of 70 CEOs who are at the top of their games. Getting behind the trappings of *The Corner Office*, Bryant identifies "indispensable lessons ... on how to lead and succeed" (subtitle of his book). He uncovers six critical qualities that will by now sound familiar to us: *passionate curiosity* (our "be resolute"); *battle-hardened confidence* (akin to our "learn confidently"); *team smarts* (our "collaborate to compete"); *a simple mindset* ("simplexity"); *fearlessness* ("learn confidently" plus); and *preparations, patience, and obstacle courses* (aspects of "do deliberatively").

Although not a perfect match, there is enough deep congruence between what Bryant discovered and what I have argued to give us confidence that our insights about the change leader hold. The key message is that practice, especially deliberative practice, drives better practice. Practice is our best bet for finding solutions and for liberating innovation. Management theorists either make the change process too complicated or simplify and generalize to the point that no specific action can be inferred. The knowledge accruing from practice-based changes is giving us the confidence of simplexity or what I refer to as "the skinny on becoming change savvy" (Fullan, 2010b). When we strip away the clutter we make change less complicated and we get at the small number of actionable items that make a bigger difference. Change then gets easier, the speed of quality implementation accelerates, and the results are more sustainable. All of this is possible because it is grounded in your practice, and what you and your colleagues are able to generate using the kind of practice-based knowledge I have identified throughout this book.

But don't expect the process to be linear or problems to be solved once and for all. There are always new issues and new people entering the situation. Your best bet is the "just right" simplexity approach—neither too simple nor too complicated. Sustain your simplexity stance and you can call yourself an accomplished change leader, which also means you are helping others to get this good. The world will be the beneficiary. Go for it!

REFERENCES

Abrahamson, E. (2004). *Change without pain*. Boston: Harvard Business School Press.

Barber, M. (2007). *Instruction to deliver*. London: Methuen.

Berry, L., & Seltman, K. (2008). *Management lessons from Mayo Clinic*. New York: McGraw-Hill.

Boyle, A. (2009). *Tower Hamlets case story*. Unpublished paper. Beyond Expectations Project, Boston College.

Bryant, A. (2011). *The corner office: Indispensable and unexpected lessons from CEOs on how to lead and succeed*. New York: Henry Holt.

Burton, R. (2008). *On being certain: Believing you are right even when you're not*. New York: St. Martin's Griffin.

Carr, N. (2010). *The shallows: What the Internet is doing to our brains*. New York: Norton.

Catholic District School Board of Eastern Ontario. (2009). *Student achievement board improvement plan, 2009–2010*. Cornwall, Ontario: Author.

Catholic District School Board of Eastern Ontario. (2010). *Strategic Plan, 2010–2013*. Cornwall, Ontario: Author.

Chabris, C., & Simons, D. (2010). *The invisible gorilla: And other ways our intuitions deceive us*. New York: Crown.

Christakis, N., & Fowler, J. (2009). *Connected: The surprising power of our social networks and how they shape our lives*. New York: Little, Brown.

Cohen, D., & Moffitt, S. (2009). *The ordeal of equality*. Cambridge, MA: Harvard University Press.

Colvin, G. (2008). *Talent is overrated*. New York: Penguin.

Crawford, M. (2009). *Shop class as soulcraft*. New York: Penguin Press.

Crutchfield, L., & McLeod Grant, H. (2007). *Forces for good: The six practices of high-impact nonprofits*. San Francisco: Jossey-Bass.

Daft, R. (2010). *The executive and the elephant*. San Francisco: Jossey-Bass.

Deutschman, A. (2009). *Walk the walk: The #1 rule for real leaders*. New York: Portfolio Books.

Doidge, N. (2007). *The brain that changes itself*. New York: Penguin.

DuFour, R. P., DuFour, R., Eaker, R., & Karhanek, G. (2009). *Raising the bar and closing the gap*. Bloomington, IN: Solution Tree.

Duggan, W. (2007). *Strategic intuition: The creative spark in human achievement*. New York: Columbia Business School Press.

Dweck, C. (2006). *Mindset: The new psychology of success*. New York: Ballantine Books.

Freedman, D. (2010). *Wrong: Why experts keep failing us—and how to know when not to trust them*. New York: Little Brown.

Fullan, M. (2001). *Leading in a culture of change*. San Francisco: Jossey-Bass.

Fullan, M. (2008). *The six secrets of change*. San Francisco: Jossey-Bass.

Fullan, M. (2010a). *All systems go*. Thousand Oaks, CA: Corwin Press.

Fullan, M. (2010b). *Motion leadership: The skinny on becoming change savvy*. Thousand Oaks, CA: Corwin Press.

Fullan, M. (2010c). *Motion leadership; the movie*. Thousand Oaks, CA: Corwin-Sinet. http://www.corwin-sinet.com/ Michael_Fullan_Info.cfm.

Fullan, M. (2011a). *The moral imperative realized*. Thousand Oaks, CA: Corwin Press.

Fullan, M. (2011b). *Choosing the wrong drivers for whole system reform*. Melbourne, Australia: Centre for Strategic Education.

Gawande, A. (2010). *The checklist manifesto: How to get things right*. New York: Metropolitan Books.

Gittell, J. (2009). *High performance healthcare*. New York: McGraw-Hill.

Goldin, C., & Katz, L. (2008). *The race between education and technology*. Cambridge, MA: Harvard University Press.

Goleman, D. (2006). *Social intelligence*. New York: Bantam Books.

Haidt, J. (2006). *The happiness hypothesis*. New York: Basic Books.

Hallinan, J. (2009). *Why we make mistakes: How we look without seeing, forget things in seconds, and are all pretty sure we are way above average*. New York: Broadway Books.

Hansen, M. (2009). *Collaboration: How leaders avoid the traps, create unity, and reap big results*. Boston: Harvard Business Press.

Hanushek, E., & Lindseth, A. (2009). *Schoolhouses, courthouses, and statehouses*. Princeton, NJ: Princeton University Press.

Heath, C., & Heath, D. (2010). *Switch: How to change things when change is hard*. New York: Broadway Books.

Heifetz, R., & Linsky, M. (2002). *Leadership on the line*. Boston: Harvard Business Press.

Herold, D., & Fedor, D. (2008). *Change the way you lead change.* Palo Alto, CA: Stanford University Press.

Hopper, K., & Hopper, W. (2009). *The Puritan gift.* New York: I. B. Tauris.

Jackson, M. (2009). *Distracted: The erosion of attention and the coming dark age.* New York: Prometheus Books.

Jacobs, C. (2010). *Management rewired.* New York: Penguin Books.

Jansen, J. (2009). *Knowledge in the blood.* Palo Alto, CA: Stanford University Press.

Johnson, S. (2010). *Where good ideas come from: The natural history of innovation.* New York: Riverhead Books.

Kluger, J. (2008). *Simplexity.* New York: Hyperion Books.

Lanier, J. (2010). *You are not a gadget: A manifesto.* New York: Knopf.

Lencioni, P. (2007). *The three signs of a miserable job.* San Francisco: Jossey-Bass.

Machiavelli, N. (1961). *The prince.* London: Penguin Books. Originally published 1515.

McLean, R. (2010). *Team work: Forging links between honesty, accountability and success.* Camberwell, Victoria, Australia: Penguin Group.

Micklethwait, J., & Wooldridge, A. (1996). *The witch doctors: What the management gurus are saying and what it means for you, your company, and your career*. New York: Times Books, Random House.

Miller, P. (2010). *The smart swarm: How understanding flocks, schools, and colonies can make us better at communicating, decision making, and getting things done*. London: Penguin Group.

Mintzberg, H. (2004). *Managers not MBAs*. San Francisco: Berrett-Koehler.

Mintzberg, H. (2009). *Managing*. San Francisco: Berrett-Koehler.

Mintzberg, H., Ahlstrand, B., & Lampel, J. (2010). *Management? It's not what you think!* New York: AMACOM.

Morrell, M., & Capparell, S. (2001). *Shackleton's way*. New York: Penguin Group.

Mortenson, G., & Relin, D. (2009). *Three cups of tea*. New York: Penguin Books.

Mourshed, M., Chinezi, C., & Barber, M. (2010). *How the world's most improved school systems keep getting better*. London: McKinsey & Co.

Oliver, J. (2005). *Jamie's school dinners* [DVD]. London: Fremantle Media.

Organisation for Economic Co-operation and Development. (2010). *PISA 2009 results*. Paris: OECD.

Pascale, R., Sternin, J., & Sternin, M. (2010). *The power of positive deviance: How unlikely innovators solve the world's toughest problems*. Boston: Harvard Business Press.

Peters, T., & Waterman, R. (1982). *In search of excellence*. New York: HarperCollins.

Pfeffer, J. (2010). *Power: Why some people have it—and others don't*. New York: HarperBusiness.

Pfeffer, J., & Sutton, R. (2000). *The knowing-doing gap*. Boston: Harvard Business School Press.

Pfeffer, J., & Sutton, R. (2006). *Hard facts, dangerous half-truths and total nonsense*. Boston: Harvard Business School Press.

Pink, D. (2009). *Drive: The surprising truth about what motivates us*. New York: Riverhead Books.

Reeves, D. (2009). *Leading change in your school*. Alexandria, VA: ASCD.

Reeves, D. (2010). *Finding your leadership focus*. New York: Teachers College Press.

Rock, D. (2009). *Your brain at work: Strategies for overcoming distraction, regaining focus, and working smarter all day long*. New York: Harper Business.

Rushkoff, D. (2010). *Program or be programmed*. New York: OR Books.

Schwartz, B., & Sharpe, K. (2010). *Practical wisdom*. New York: Riverhead Books, Penguin.

Senge, P. (1990). *The fifth discipline: The art and practice of the learning organization*. New York: Doubleday.

Sharp, I. (2009). *Four Seasons: The story of a business philosophy*. Toronto, Ontario: Penguin Group.

Sharratt, L., & Fullan, M. (2009). *Realization*. Thousand Oaks, CA: Corwin Press.

Stewart, M. (2009). *The management myth: Why the "experts" keep getting it wrong*. New York: Norton.

Sutton, R. (2010). *Good boss, bad boss: How to be the best and learn from the worst*. New York: Business Plus.

Tavris, C., & Aronson, E. (2007). *Mistakes were made (but not by me): Why we justify foolish beliefs, bad decisions, and hurtful acts*. New York: Harcourt.

Taylor, W., & LaBarre, P. (2006). *Mavericks at work*. New York. William Morrow.

Tennyson, R. (2003). *The partnering toolbook*. London: International Business Leaders Forum.

Thurmon, D. (2010). *Off balance on purpose: Embrace uncertainty and create a life you love*. Austin, TX: Greenleaf Book Group.

Wheatley, M. (2006). *Leadership and the new science*. San Francisco: Berrett-Koehler.

INDEX